at home
SARAH STYLE

Published by Simon & Schuster
New York London Toronto Sydney New Delhi

Simon & Schuster Canada
A Division of Simon & Schuster, Inc.
166 King Street East, Suite 300
Toronto, Ontario, M5A 1J3

Untitled by Tom Hodgson (pg 1). Reprinted by permission of the estate of Tom Hodgson.
Beach by Molly Lamb Bobak (pgs 6, 39). Reprinted by permission of Alex Bobak.
Eternal Hexagon by Robert Indiana (pgs 10, 38). © 2015 Morgan Art Foundation / Artists Rights Society (ARS),
  New York / SODRAC.
BB6 by Dean West (pg 18). Reprinted by permission of Dean West.
Friday Morning by Jack Bush (pg 21). © Estate of Jack Bush / SODRAC (2015).
Assembly of Square Forms (pg 22), a screenprint of 1969 by Barbara Hepworth © Bowness.
Untitled circa 1986 by Patrick Landsley (pg 23). Reprinted by permission of Patrick Landsley.
Weaver Vermilion by Michael Adamson (pg 36). Reprinted by permission of Michael Adamson.
Homage to the Square: Saturation by Josef Albers (pg 37). © Estate of Josef Albers / SODRAC (2015).
Sky's the Limit by Susan Wallis (pg 156). Reprinted by permission of Susan Wallis.
Peony #2 by Susan Straiton (pg 157). Reprinted by permission of Susan Straiton.

This Simon & Schuster Canada edition November 2015.

SIMON & SCHUSTER CANADA and colophon are registered trademarks of Simon & Schuster, Inc.

For information about special discounts for bulk purchases, please contact
Simon & Schuster Special Sales at 1-800-268-3216 or CustomerService@simonandschuster.ca.

Library and Archives Canada Cataloguing in Publication

Richardson, Sarah, 1971–, author
  At home : Sarah style / Sarah Richardson.

Issued in print and electronic formats.

   1. Richardson, Sarah, 1971– —Homes and haunts—Ontario.   2. Interior decorators—Homes and haunts—Ontario.
3. Interior decorators—Homes and haunts—Ontario—Pictorial works.   4. Interior decoration—Ontario.
I. Title.   II. Title: Sarah style.

NK2115.3.I57R52 2015   747.09713   C2015-903854-5   C2015-903855-3

Interior design by Rose Pereira
Jacket design by Rose Pereira
Jacket photography by Stacey Brandford
Room photography by Stacey Brandford
Additional room photography by Michael Graydon, Mark Olson, and Bjorn Wallander
Front cover painting by Michael Adamson

Manufactured in the United States of America

10 9 8 7 6 5 4 3 2 1

ISBN 978-1-5011-1949-1
ISBN 978-1-5011-1950-7 (ebook)

DEDICATION

This is dedicated to my husband, Alexander Younger. Without you, this would be a very short book. Your support is unwavering, your zest for life is unmatched, and as a result, our life at home is an exciting adventure. Thanks for encouraging me to tackle the next blank canvas with you and making me always happy to be home.

1

18

120

94

70

148

168

7
6
5
4
3
2
1

202

238

FROM MY HOUSE
TO YOURS

The book you hold is my personal portrait of everyday
life. This is a combination of design and food and my own
snapshots, presented together to offer my take on life at
home, Sarah style. I've often said design is like a recipe.
A home is essentially a mix of ingredients that, when
combined, create a finished product. Like cooking, design
is an experiment — sometimes you savour the results,
and other times you wonder where the recipe went
wrong. Not every room and not every meal I've made is a
masterpiece, but there is a sameness with which I approach
the design of interior spaces and the life we live at home,
and I would describe it this way: I have an appreciation
for simple yet wholesome elements, prefer materials and
flavours that are fresh and pure and authentic regardless of
their provenance or price, and believe that homes and meals
are meant to be experienced and shared daily and not saved
for special occasions. These are the spaces I live or have
lived in with my family, accompanied by a glimpse of what
is often cooking in our kitchens. Seasonally inspired, simply
prepared, and family tested. This is my life at home, and
these are our recipes. Come in, get comfortable, and enjoy.
Thanks for stopping by!

Sarah

Alexander and I had started talking about taking the big leap and buying a house together. We each had our own house, and neither place ticked all the proverbial boxes for the other person. So, we did what all modern couples do and dipped our toes to test the waters with an online search. Instead of touring countless houses, we instantly landed on "the one." I had moved six times in the previous five years and looked at each new home as a temporary stepping-stone until something better presented itself, but this house was different.

A modern, international-style home on a ravine setting in a prime neighbourhood (and at a price we could afford) was tantamount to winning the lottery. As with any house purchase and subsequent renovation, there were challenges and pitfalls, but I quickly learned that there would be no next move, because this was clearly our "forever." Of course, you know the rest of the story . . . there was a wedding, two kids, a puppy, some fish, and a family was made.

CITY
MODERN

Just because you love someone doesn't mean you have the same taste — in each other, yes . . . but in design, maybe not. Alexander loves bold colour, and I have always gravitated to a light palette. What's the solution? If you design in neutrals for all the big-ticket furnishing items such as upholstery and window coverings, you can add impact and colour with accessories, art, and textile accents. Covering everything in the same light, neutral palette will also allow maximum flexibility to temper the look of the room and suit your current style mood. Who says you can't always get what you want?

↑ FINDING HARMONY

Vintage mid-century elements are mixed with contemporary furnishings with clean lines to highlight the rectilinear architecture of the building. A quiet palette of materials allows you to read the interior and the architecture as a cohesive and harmonious whole.

MOODY ROOMS

In the early days of living in our house, we only ever used our dining room in the evening for entertaining, so I chose a rich and earthy scheme. The deep olive walls and matching velvet drapes provide a cool contrast to the warmth of rich, natural woods used on the furniture and floors. When designing your dining room, think about how and when you'll use it, and tailor the style to fit your lifestyle.

THE DESIGN LAB

As a designer, my job is to devise creative solutions for other people's homes. To provide the best advice and service, I've always believed that I should experiment with ideas in my own environment. As a result, our home has always been a testing ground for my latest idea. The hazard of being married to a designer is that you never know what the house will look like the next time you come home. (Alexander has often said that he checks to make sure the furniture is in the same place before he sits down!) Since all the major fixed elements, such as the cabinetry, counters, and floor, in this kitchen are neutral, I've been able to change it up with paint and accessories numerous times over a decade. It started as aubergine, then transitioned to pale aqua before becoming boldly blue. If you've got a light foundation, change is easy, so keep that in mind before you sign off on that work order for kitchen cabinets in a daring colour.

PAINTERLY EFFECT

I know it's often said that you should never match your art to your décor, but . . . I was so inspired by the joyful colours in this beach-scene painting by Molly Lamb Bobak that I wanted to carry the cheery vibe down onto the storage credenza, so I painted the frame of this vintage teak piece in glossy white and colour-blocked the doors and drawers for a hit of family-friendly fun in the hall. I say making your own rules is more fun than living by others'. Dare to do it!

TV rooms are an invitation to kick back and just chill out, so I opted to make ours the ultimate chill-out room. The double chaise is the most welcoming spot to flop after a long day, or a great place to pile in for a family movie night. The velvet upholstery may look precious for a family space, but if you upholster with cotton velvet, you can remove the covers and throw them in the washing machine so they always look good as new.

← CHILD'S PLAY

I'm drawn to playful elements for the family room that are kid friendly, yet stylish too. The overscaled zigzag print adds impact to the windows with graphic punch, the Heriz carpet is indestructible yet soft to play on, and the furniture layout leaves lots of open space for playing and spreading out.

↓ WHITE ON

You may think white is anything but childproof . . . but I will disagree. The sofa cushions have been washed and bleached many times and always look good as new, and the vintage Saarinen coffee table has a laminate top that can be scrubbed clean no matter what gets drawn on it. White is all right!

CRAFT CENTRAL

I struggled with various solutions to make the back wall of the family room work, then finally decided it needed to become a storage hub combined with a place for the girls to do arts and crafts. A multitude of drawers allows for easy organization of all manner of art supplies, toys, and dress-up costumes (at a level they can reach), and the tall pantry cupboards on either end offer flexible storage for everything from seasonal items to file boxes, all neatly hidden behind closed doors. If you use in-stock cabinets and easy-to-install butcher-block counters, a transformation like this can be done in a weekend. Enamel knobs reinforce the cheery cherry colour scheme.

THE GREAT WALL

One of my best styling tricks has always been to group all like things together, and the same principle can be applied to art. Instead of sprinkling little bitty framed pieces throughout the house, I grouped them all together and hung them in two long rows. Individually, none of the pieces is that spectacular, but many hold sentimental value. In this case, the whole is certainly greater than the sum of its parts from a decorative perspective.

← WAKE-UP CALL

After years of living in a quiet and pale bedroom, I decided to change it up and experiment with a riot of colour. Grapefruit, citrine, and peony pink made it feel as if I were waking up in a spring garden every day.

↑ INSPIRED BY ART

The painting reflected in the mirror served as inspiration for the accents in this room. Vibrant turquoise, leafy green, and pale lavender added pretty hits to an otherwise subdued scheme of cream. Be on the lookout for vintage lighting and art glass if you're aiming to add some zing to your rooms.

WONDROUS WOODS

My admiration for pattern knows no bounds, so
to make our less-than-grand-size bathroom feel
special, I indulged in luxurious materials. The door
fronts on the vanity are magnificent book-matched
panels of burled walnut, the vanity wall is covered from
floor to ceiling in penny-round marble mosaic, and the
sconces are vintage Murano glass. No matter how
small the space is, a few special details can elevate
it to new heights.

↑ ROCK A BYE

The arrival of our first child, Robin, meant turning a guest room into the nursery. Unable to find a nursery rocker with clean, modern lines, I decided to design my own and soon discovered that you can install a rocker/swivel mechanism to the base of almost any upholstered chair frame. Suddenly the design possibilities were endless!

↖ BABY MAKES THREE

I kept the custom walnut shelves that used to serve as bedside tables and designed a dresser/change table to match them. The open cubbies on the dresser proved handy spots to store diapers, and the change pad was easily removed when no longer needed.

↗ HOW THE GARDEN GROWS

Looking to capture the spirit and imagination of children's storybooks, I asked a decorative painter to trace the sinuous branches and bursting blooms on the floral fabric I chose for the rocker and transform them into a small mural on the wall. You might normally consider a mural to be a traditional application, but if you start with the right contemporary inspiration, it can be anything but old-fashioned.

Time flies. One minute you're setting up house for the first time, and the next thing you know almost fifteen years have passed. Granted these have been busy years, filled with building careers, putting down roots, and having a family. Through all the big life changes, one thing remained constant, and that's our love for the place we call home. The longer we're here, the better it gets, and it seems as if the first decade and a half were just the beginning of the story. We are caretakers of a unique house designed by a talented female architect more than a half century ago. It's not for everyone, but it's perfectly us. What started as a simple fix of the roof and windows morphed into a back-to-the-blocks renovation with the goal of keeping everything terrific about the original design while refreshing, reimagining, and preparing it for the next fifty.

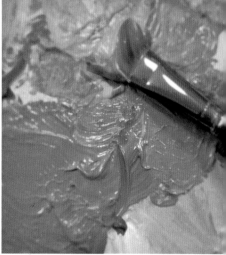

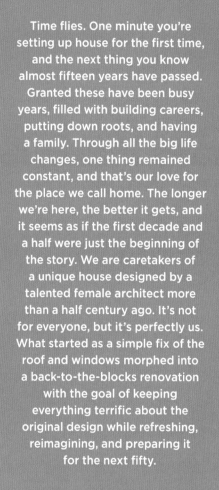
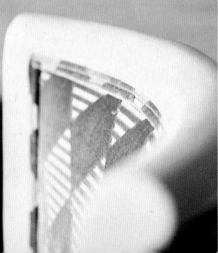

NOW

CITY MODERN

↖ MODERN WELCOME

Even a contemporary home needs to have a sense of personality, so our front door is painted a cheery and welcoming shade of robin's egg blue. The doors throughout the house were designed with horizontal bands within vertical side rails as a nod to the strong horizontal lines that dominate the architecture.

↑ YOU HAD ME AT HELLO

The two-storey wall of glass in the stairwell that is revealed the minute you open the door is a powerful architectural feature. I will never forget the moment we first saw the house with our real estate agent and how overcome I was by the light streaming in from the west and the uninterrupted sightline through the house.

↑ SKYLIGHT

Both in the original design of the house and in the new renovation, skylights are used strategically to draw natural daylight inside. Never underestimate the difference a simple skylight can make in a room.

THE POWER OF TWO

On one side of the living room sit classic Tizio task lamps atop mid-century teak and marble tables (updated with painted white bases), and a pair of vintage cantilevered Milo Baughman chairs flank the vintage tubular table. Looking for iconic modern-design furniture is a fun treasure hunt, but you'll have to look past some pretty wacky fabrics (the chairs were covered in orange and brown velour before getting the Cinderella treatment in this pale chenille).

I don't design living rooms just for entertaining. I want spaces for everyday living that draw you in and create an experience. This groovy 1970s lounger by Milo Baughman attracted me with its curvy lines and floating design, but superior comfort trumps it all and guarantees someone is always stretched out reading, chilling, or just daydreaming.

MIX MASTER

All the furnishings in the house are a mix of vintage finds with contemporary elements, but even the new pieces are designed to blend with the old, like this tailored Parsons-style sofa that I had made with a plinth base to give it a lift so that it floats visually in the room. The chevron motif in the vintage mirror is echoed in the zigzag embroidery on the pillow as well as in the matching wool carpet.

The double-sided fireplace has always been a powerful component of the layout and has become the anchor of the living room and library thanks to the dramatic veining of the Calacatta marble that now wraps around all four sides. The whimsical (and interactive) Ingo Maurer paper chandelier previously hung in the dining room and is now mirrored by a twin on the other side of the living room.

NATURAL BEAUTY

To connect the interior to the exterior, old windows were swapped out for giant lift-and-slide doors that span the entire width and height of the room. Perhaps one of the strongest architectural elements of the original house design is the liberal use of glass; the rooms are always bathed in natural light.

FLOW THROUGH

With open-concept rooms, continuity is key. The stepped tile pattern flows seamlessly from the entry hall through the kitchen in a combination of French Blue Savoy marble accented with bands of white Calacatta marble. The counter stools are covered in durable (and wipeable) grey leather with natural-walnut bases that match the dining tabletop in the adjacent space.

PERSONAL SPACE

Since our kitchen counter has long been the kids'
go-to place for colouring, drawing, and homework,
the overhang is outfitted with shallow drawers where
they store supplies. A bank of drawers on the end
keeps table linens close at hand for quick table-setting
at mealtimes. The perimeter of the kitchen is pure
white, and the island cabinetry is a whisper of grey.

→ BACK TO THE FUTURE

The sleek and modern pendant lights
are a reissued design dating back to
the '50s from Danish manufacturer
Louis Poulsen. Kitchen pendants may
be a small detail but they have huge
impact in the overall design of your
renovation. It took me a year to finally
find these, and I'm glad I waited to
find the perfect match.

NEVER GIVE UP

Like many, I always dreamed of having
a giant island as the anchor for cooking,
entertaining, and family life in the kitchen.
But it never worked with the original house
layout. The driving force for our renovation
was to make the house live up to its full
potential and work in "forever" terms.
To get better space and use out of the
cooking and eating areas, we reconfigured
the powder room and front-hall closet
to enable an open-concept kitchen
and dining room. It was less difficult
to achieve than I imagined, and the new
configuration is next-level awesome.
It's always worth investigating before
you deem anything impossible.

MOTHER NATURE AS ARTIST

The durability and carefree maintenance of quartz counters is unbeatable for surfaces that get a lot of wear and tear, so I opted for practicality on all the main surface counters, then splurged on a statement slab of Calacatta marble to wrap up the backsplash for the range and across the raised china cabinet that serves as a visual divider (and display area) at the end of the island.

↑ LET IT FLOW

For the sleekest lines and most durable end gables in a high-traffic kitchen, we treated the ends of the counter runs to waterfall edges. The white quartz counters are mitred and wrap down to the floor, which can make for a challenging installation but also a happy chef and lasting results.

→ DOMESTIC GODDESS

My six-burner gas range was the first thing I committed to in the kitchen. Packed with power and ready to deliver delicious results, this gorgeous range was a good investment that delivers daily dividends.

← **ARTFUL
TREASURES**

An open display shelf
illuminated by LED strip
lighting punctuates a
full-height wall of pantry
cupboards to project
a pretty vista as you
approach the house.
If you have a collection
of handcrafted treasures
you've gathered over
time, be sure to place
them where you can
celebrate them daily.

→ **GARDEN**

A handy porch off the
kitchen that's elevated
off the street makes
barbecuing a breeze and
feels as if you were in an
adult tree house. Since
we grown-ups aren't
quite so enamoured with
sitting cross-legged on
the ground, our little
lounge is decked out
with a grouping of the
reissued iconic '50s
Acapulco chair in funky
kelly green. It's perfect
for kicking back on
summer nights.

THE BIG FIX

Truth be told, our dining room had become that room that was rarely used, and I jokingly called it "shipping and receiving," since things were always coming and going but nothing was ever right enough to stay. It just felt dark and segregated from the rest of the house and had no energy. Opening the dining room to the kitchen and replacing the wall of the hall with a sleek glass railing completely transformed our formally forlorn dining room. The chandelier was salvaged from a local hotel ballroom built at the same time as the house. The palm-leaf print on the drapes references our leafy view, and I designed the table and chairs with a nod to mod styling. In a room filled with quiet elements, the art takes centre stage, upping the colour quotient.

← SHAKEN, NOT STIRRED

One of the all-time coolest elements of the original house layout was a hidden bar that often went totally unnoticed behind a hinged bookshelf. It was seriously funky, but it was also a bit cramped during a party (I think it had a maximum occupancy of two), so we rethought the room, said goodbye to the James Bond bar, and ended up with a convergence of three great features: a library, a bar, and a den. It may no longer be a secret, but it sure makes a great escape.

↑ THROW IT BACK

Floating cabinetry on the bar and wraparound bookshelves in the library (complete with pullout tabletops) are made of whitewashed white oak, while the bar back is wrapped in antiqued mirror and the bar peninsula forms a cube of onyx thanks to mitred seams that allow the stone to wrap continuously around the cabinetry. Brushed-brass fixtures and accessories keep the vintage vibe alive.

GEO DETAIL

The staggered stone pattern in the hall transitions to a sharp geometric in the powder room that was achieved by slicing twelve-by-twelve-inch tiles into scalene triangles with outer dimensions of six by twelve inches. Be sure you're on very good terms with your tilesetter before you propose this idea, as it takes patience and precision to pull it off. But it's well worth the effort (so says the girl who didn't have to install it). Palm-tree wallpaper, brushed-brass hardware, and a wraparound marble vanity with antiqued mirror door fronts all give this pint-size room lots of panache.

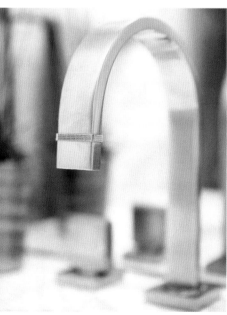

CLOUD NINE

I've decorated my share of bright and bold bedrooms, but this
is the antithesis of them all. Dressed all in white and cream with a tiny
nod to sky blues, this room is so restful and serene that I imagine it to
be like the inside of a cloud. With a plush channel-tufted bed, a pair of
linen-covered, vintage Robsjohn-Gibbings chairs, teak bedside tables,
and mid-century bedside lights, this room matches the mood of
the misty landscape that hangs over the long, low dresser.

CLOSET CONFIDENTIAL

In the same way that reorienting the kitchen redefined our use and enjoyment of it, so too did flipping our bathroom and closet have a domino effect of pure pleasure. I happily said goodbye to our not-quite-a-walk-in closet and hello to a single wall of floor-to-ceiling built-ins. In the end we netted more storage in the bedroom as well as a much bigger bathroom that includes a double vanity and a separate tub and shower. It may take a lot of crumpled plans to finally reach a goal and get everything you want out of the rooms in your house, but playing with the puzzle until every piece fits is a most rewarding game.

BATHING BEAUTY

The herringbone pattern on the bathroom floor was made from twelve-by-twenty-four-inch Calacatta marble tiles that were cut into six-by-twenty-four-inch strips and installed in alternating honed and polished bands for subtle contrast. The vanity is treated in the same vein with a frame in matte finish and doors and drawers in high gloss.

SOAK IT UP

The bathtub and counters are covered in Namib Sky
marble that captures the look of clouds drifting by. The
wall-to-wall mirror with vintage Italian glass sconces
enhances the light and airy feeling, while a waterfall
showerhead completes the feel of a total escape.

MOD SQUAD

In our youngest daughter Fiona's room, vintage treasures abound. The teak bed with built-in side tables got a new lease on life with a fresh spray of powdery aqua paint, as did the base of a vintage saucerlike lounger (formerly dressed in the scratchiest brown plaid upholstery, it bears no resemblance to its pre-makeover self). Zigzags, dots, and Dalmatian spots help channel a spirit that is youthful yet not juvenile, and the bold geometric wall treatment was a quick and easy paint project achieved with a roll of painter's masking tape and three quarts of paint. The best part about a pattern like this is that it takes minutes to tape it up, and you can instantly see if you like what you've designed before you commit the time and paint to make it permanent.

DRESS ME UP

Formerly dark-orangey teak with a black plinth and black leather handles, this simple dresser showcases the beauty of a subtle paint palette with a powdery aqua frame and glossy white drawer fronts. The glass handles are easy to grab, and the low profile is ideally suited to keeping everything in reach for the littlest lady in our house. The streamlined profile and smooth finish of teak furniture combined with the accessible price point of vintage pieces make finds like this ideal candidates for a makeover in my book. Just avoid painting anything that's been treated with teak oil, as the paint may not adhere as well.

SCRUB-A-DUB

A wall-to-wall white oak vanity is
flanked by vintage sconces with
green glass covers and accented with
a jaunty geometric marble backsplash
in Ming Green. Sporty racing stripes
in the same Ming Green marble flank
the white marble on the floor, then
wrap continuously up the face of the
bathtub and through the shower.

SCHOOL RULES

For my girl who loves to draw, this bathroom is an homage to graph
paper. The vanity pattern was mapped out to disguise the space between
the doors and drawers so it forms a uniform grid, while the floor pattern was
laid with narrow mosaic bands wrapping around twenty-four-inch-square
Carrara marble to create a high-contrast border. A hint of pink gives a
feminine nod to the peppy pink that adorns her adjacent bedroom
in a style that is anything but subtle.

SLEEPING BEAUTY

I couldn't help myself when I discovered this amazing flamingo wallpaper. One wall just wouldn't do it, and I went bananas and turned Robin's bedroom into a veritable bird sanctuary (with full permission, of course, because the number one rule for decorating kids' rooms is to involve them and make them feel it really is their private little escape from the big and wild world). In the previous incarnation of the room, walnut shelves soared from floor to ceiling. These were replaced with a pair of closets faced in floor-to-ceiling mirrors that flank a retro dresser I had nabbed at an auction for a bargain. The bed is made from a simple upholstered wall-mount panel, and the box spring is supported on painted decorative feet for a super simple and space-saving solution.

CANDY FLOSS

It's great to be girlie, but you've got to know where to stop. Bold geometric sheets, carpet, and upholstery choices keep this room from being too sticky-sweet.

CHAIR PAIR

The chairs in the girls' bedrooms both share the same '60s provenance.
I bought them from the same vintage dealer, and they were dressed in
the same bad plaid suit. Here, scrubbed up with its legs painted white and
re-covered in the same soft neutral fabric that's on the bed, this throwback
beauty can now be appreciated for her shapely silhouette.

FLOWER POWER

A pair of vintage modern nightstands was reimagined from mustardy yellow to high-gloss geranium pink, and the scuffed brass hardware was replated in shiny nickel.

3:19.

PHILIPS

UPSTAIRS DOWNSTAIRS

The original stairs were replaced with a new floating staircase with glass panels and open treads. Access to the guest room/home office was reoriented to create better flow from the main areas and draw natural light into both the bedroom and adjacent hall that used to hold our gallery wall (pg 11).

↓ A FINE VINTAGE

Finding just the right way to add a modern edge to a not-too-grand wine cellar was no easy task. Thanks to the easy-to-assemble modular aluminum wine-racking system that mimics a beehive design, our vintages now compose an orderly graphic presentation that's backlit with LED lights for dramatic effect and on display through a clear glass door with matching aluminum framing.

→ THE LITTLE DETAILS

While working on a project in England, I was introduced to their sleek and sexy light switches and cover plates, and could not fathom why we North Americans had to settle for such ho-hum alternatives. And then to my absolute delight I discovered they were available here! You may wonder how anyone could get so enthused over toggle switches and simple rotary dials, but these really do make a difference, and I'm amazed at how many people have commented about our light switches and door hardware. In any renovation, as Charles Eames said, "The details aren't just the details. They make the design." Smart man.

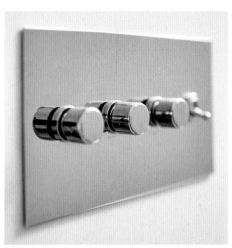

SWEET DREAMS

To instill an aura of tranquility, the guest room is clad in a muted palette.
The neutral palette is infused with tactile touches such as a wall-to-wall
headboard, plush velvet upholstery fabrics, and a woven grasscloth wall.
As long as little feet don't run in to give you an early wake-up call,
it should be peaceful slumbers in here.

CALL THE OFFICE

Sometimes we need a quiet place to work at home, and sometimes we need a guest room. We don't ever need them both on the same day, and we don't have a house full of guests often enough to prioritize one over the other, so our decision was to combine and conquer. A long desk tucks neatly under a wide window to give any time spent working at home an inspiring outlook.

PLAYTIME

Since buying the house nearly fifteen years ago, we always struggled with the massive granite wall that lined the playroom on the lower level. Luckily we're set into a hill, so we get the bonus of big windows even on the lower level, but the wall was so overpowering that I simply could not decorate around it, and eventually bid it goodbye (more like good riddance) during the renovation. With white walls and a pared-down layout accented with energetic, kid-friendly fabric patterns, this family playroom works for the whole gang from day through night. The tub chairs are on swivel bases — ideal for movie watching — and the airy profile of the tables and lamps don't block the sunlight from streaming on in.

HANGING OUT

If one side of the playroom is designed for family time, the other side, accordingly, needs to be focused on play. I fondly remember enjoying the hanging basket chair in my aunt and uncle's house as a child, and jumped for joy when I discovered a reissued version right when I was tackling this renovation. Less expensive and more fun than a standard-issue armchair, these swinging rattan options make playtime fun time. Wall-to-wall storage is punctuated with a built-in daybed and bookshelf that gives the kids a comfy spot to nest (or rest).

ARTIST IN RESIDENCE

Our former laundry room hogged a big window, leaving a long, dark hallway. We bid adieu to that ugly old space and, in knocking out the wall, ushered in a transformation into a dynamite, creative studio for building, playing, and tackling projects. The cabinets are colour-blocked in four pastel hues of blue and green and contain all the art and office supplies.

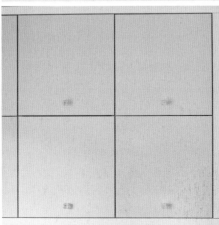

GARDEN GLORY

Outdoor living in Canada is geared for enjoying the good weather whenever possible. Our game-changing renovation plan was to replace walls of windows with giant lift and slide doors that blur the boundaries between indoors and out and make everyday entertaining a breeze. The wirework chairs combine the lyrical spirit of '50s design with modern production for a fun and funky alternative to traditional patio furniture. We discovered these while travelling in Italy, but they were too big to bring home. I was ecstatic to discover I could get them shipped directly to our garden.

It all started with an afternoon drive in an old car on a fall weekend afternoon. We found ourselves on a charming dirt road, just minutes from the farm we designed and built for *Sarah's House* on HGTV. We had no intention of moving on from the farm we had built and loved, but we soon found ourselves head over heels for a new property full of potential with breathtaking views. Saying goodbye to that beautiful farm meant starting anew on a different adventure, and we set about turning the existing, dated '80s bungalow into a country-style family retreat while thinking about building our dream home on a different part of the property. Renovated with budget-friendly building supplies — filled with charm thanks to a mix of architectural salvage and flea-market finds — this house proves that you can achieve winning style when you use everyday materials in innovative ways. Four years later, we're still dreaming about the dream house, while we enjoy every single minute right where we are.

COUNTRY HOME

STARLIGHT
FARM

↖ ORDER IN THE HOUSE

Country life comes with lots of gear and plenty of layers for all that outdoor living. To keep a sense of order by the back door (and to encourage the little ones to take part in keeping everything off the floor), I installed sturdy double hooks at staggered levels that can hold a pile of coats while keeping them ready to grab when running out the door.

↖ SHELF LIFE

Painted shelves made from pine lumber and ready-made brackets help increase the amount of gear this petite area can gobble up. Baskets labelled with each of our names hold hats, mitts, and other accessories, and the bench offers a perch for pulling on boots. The bench also allows us to tuck a couple of rows of shoes underneath, which means not tripping over them as you come in the door.

← BEHIND CLOSED DOORS

We're a family of winter-sports enthusiasts, which translates into an abundance of skis, boots, helmets, and outerwear. Knowing how much room all this consumes, I decided to convert the spacious furnace room into a storage-laden mudroom. Instead of one big shared closet, I bought ready-made six-panel pine doors and framed them up individually so each has a dedicated use (or owner). If you're looking to brighten a subterranean space, paint the doors in a fun accent colour for a bit of punch.

↑ DOMINO EFFECT

The main living spaces here are all combined into one room, so a unified palette was needed throughout. In an effort to make the room live as large as possible, I opted to dress every surface in the same calm tones so your eye would just drift across the room without being interrupted by bold pattern or colour that yells out "look at me."

↑ TABLE TALK

Casual living calls for a coffee table that does it all. I like to be able to pile up books and magazines, fill a vase with freshly picked flowers, and still have room to set out hors d'oeuvres when entertaining. At three feet by five feet, this one is the anchor of the action in the living room. It's made from salvaged porch-railing spindles I bought for a few dollars each and was whipped up by our carpenter in under an hour. Topped with a remnant piece of marble, this is the epitome of feet-up, laid-back living.

↗ FABULOUS FOCAL

This mantel is an assemblage of salvaged trim pieces from local buildings. The wide piece beneath the top was actually a single run of baseboard that I bought for just twenty dollars from a historic house. The corbel brackets have their original chipped and crackled paint finish, lending an authentic touch.

↓ FLEA MARKET FINDS

I'm often asked where I find all the vintage and antique elements I use in my design projects. I frequently visit consignment shops, estate auctions, and vintage furniture dealers, but if time and schedule permit, I like to blitz the project at a big outdoor antique show in a single day. I start by making a list of everything we are looking for, organized by each room (with pertinent dimensions if a piece needs to be a specific size), and tick it off as I go along. The botanicals on the walls were five dollars each, and the chandelier, ceramics, accent tables, and accessories were assembled from different dealers at the same show. Talk about a worthwhile one-stop shop!

↙ BUDGET BASICS

Not knowing exactly where each piece of upholstered furniture might end up in the house, I opted for maximum flexibility and bought the same budget-friendly oyster twill to go on just about everything. You can't beat the durability of basic twill (think about how hardwearing it is for pants), and it's easy to dress up with a pretty pillow. In my world you don't have to be expensive to be fabulous.

ONE-STOP SHOP

I'm never one to shy away from a challenge. For a series of online videos I produced for my website, I wanted to see what results could be achieved by renovating a house strictly with supplies available from a big-box store. Not everyone has access to all the resources I have living in a big city with great design shops, so I thought this would be a universally appealing idea. The only elements from other sources are things you can't buy at a "big box," such as the stools, dining chairs and table, and accessories. This house is proof positive that it's not about where you shop that counts, it's how you use what you find!

When installing a decorative backsplash, order enough
to tile right up to the underside of the vent hood. It's
practical for cooking messes, but it also allows you
to get extra visual impact, since the backsplash will be
installed at eye level and be visible from all angles
of the kitchen.

⤢ DISH DUTY

Even a small kitchen can benefit from having a second sink. It allows you to have another prep and cleanup station so there can easily be more cooks in the kitchen. Instead of the typical small, rectangular bar sink, an eighteen-inch round sink can handle a large pot for cleanup and offers better multifunctional use. Plus, since most elements in your kitchen are big and boxy (such as appliances and cabinetry), a round element helps break up the sharp angles.

↑ SHUTTER AND SHAKER

To create a loosely layered look, I combined two different door profiles. A plain Shaker-style door is well suited to the lower cabinetry, while a decorative shutter-style upper door has a country-casual feel (and has the same Shaker panel around the perimeter so the two styles complement each other). When mixing two door profiles in two colours, you'll need to carefully choose what goes where. For continuity, it usually looks best to select the upper-cabinetry colour and profile for any full-height pantry cupboards, as well as the gables beside the refrigerator.

→ TABLE TALK

When laying out a kitchen, you need to design what works best for your lifestyle. This built-in banquette has extra storage cabinets beneath the seat and towers of drawers that anchor the ends (for the girls' art supplies on one end and table linens on the other). The seat is covered in leather, which has proven to be an excellent choice for even the messiest little hands. With compact room proportions, a built-in banquette makes the most of all available space, and more important, it's a cozy place to hang out in the hub of the house!

← FAMILY GATHERING

It's hard to imagine, but at one time this family room was dressed in a wolverine wallpaper border and suffered from water damage and mildew. Since the house is built into a hill, this lower space is blessed with full-height windows, and plenty of light streams in.

↙ WALNUT WOW

Thanks to modern innovation, you can take your rumpus room up a notch and install engineered hardwood flooring directly on top of your concrete basement floor. This wide-plank, prefinished walnut floor costs less than broadloom and lends an air of elegance to the entire lower level. While the upper level is pale and silvery, this lower room has textured grasscloth walls, crewel-embroidered drapes, rustic rattan chairs, and a rich palette of warm woods and pinky reds.

FOLLOW THE LEADER

I can't say I was looking for a traditional carved-oak four-poster bed, but when I found
this beauty in a consignment shop at an incredibly low price, I simply had to bring it home.
To keep it from feeling too stuffy and fancy in our simple little home, I took a page from British
Colonial style and layered in casual elements in humble materials such as the caned side chairs
and faux-bamboo table, armoire, and bedside tables. The mix of painted furniture and wood
keeps the room feeling light and bright, casual, and true to its country roots.

HELLO, SUNSHINE

Soon after we took possession of the house, spring arrived, and up through the ground popped a garden filled with daffodils, planted by the former owner's late wife. The girls started referring to it as "the daffodil house." When it came time to choose a direction for each room, I was reminded of how happy and cheery a field of yellow looks after a long, cold winter and decided a sunny-yellow guest room would be warm and welcoming for visitors no matter what the weather outside.

STAR LIGHT, STAR BRIGHT

We named the property Starlight Farm as a tribute to the incredibly dark night skies we are blessed to enjoy here. Away from the light pollution of nearby cities, we are able to indulge in the magic of starry skies at night. I was craving a palette of rich blue hues in the bedroom but didn't want to sacrifice light for colour, so I installed a chair rail all around the room and painted the lower section in inky blue, while washing the upper section in the softest cream. This treatment offers the best of both worlds if you're looking to have it all . . . which I always am!

↑ DESIGNER TOUCH

Here's a little small-world story. Before Tommy Smythe worked with me on our TV shows and design projects, his mentor was John Manuel, a well-known Toronto designer who worked in many of the city's best homes. In the 1950s he designed the Les Touches fabric pattern, shown here on the chairs and pillows, for Brunschwig & Fils. As Zelina Brunschwig wisely said, "Good design is forever," and I think this fabric is a testament to that truth. More than sixty years after it was first designed, this pattern looks fresh and modern and now.

TRUE BLUE

In the girls' bedroom, the chair-rail trim profile was moved up the wall and installed twenty-one inches below the ceiling. Since standard wallpaper rolls are twenty-one inches wide and twenty-seven feet long, two rolls of wallpaper, used sideways, were enough to add a pretty patterned touch to the upper section of their bedroom walls. The lower section was painted the same colour as the printed pattern, and all the bedding, fabrics, and carpet tie into the scheme.

SPACE SAVING

A narrow space doesn't limit your ability to use a decorative sconce. Instead of placing a single sconce above the mirror, you can install a pair of sconces on the side walls of a narrow powder room. These galvanized outdoor sconces wash the walls with light and provide ample illumination while allowing you to opt for a design that brings a touch of whimsy to a functional space.

BUNKING IN

Overnight guests are a given in the country, and making room for everyone is a must. Since the focus is on outdoor activities, there's no need for huge bedrooms. This was an unfinished storage room before we converted it into a funky bunkroom. The walls are papered in topographical maps of the area so the kids can explore their surroundings.

NIGHT LIGHTS

The bunks are simply crafted from painted pine from the lumber store and the ladder is vintage salvage from a local store. Little metal reading lights are durable enough to survive a pillow fight and allow the kids to decide when it's really time for lights-out.

In Canada we are blessed with an abundance of beautiful, remote, freshwater lakes carved through the Canadian Shield. As a kid I grew up visiting my grandparents' cottages, exploring the lake by canoe or 9.9-horsepower "tin can," buying penny candy, swimming constantly, and playing with my many cousins. It was heaven! I now spend my summers in the open water of Georgian Bay, thanks to my husband, Alexander, who nabbed a tiny little island in the days before we became "us." Almost ten years later, we made some changes to our little island getaway to make it work for our expanding family and friends, documenting the process for my *Sarah's Cottage* series on HGTV while I was in my third trimester with our second daughter. There are many different interpretations of cottage living, and each has its own charm. Whether it's a cabin in the woods or a grand estate, there is no singular definition of what makes a cottage. One element is constant, though — a cottage is where we Canadians go to enjoy the all-too-brief magic of summer.

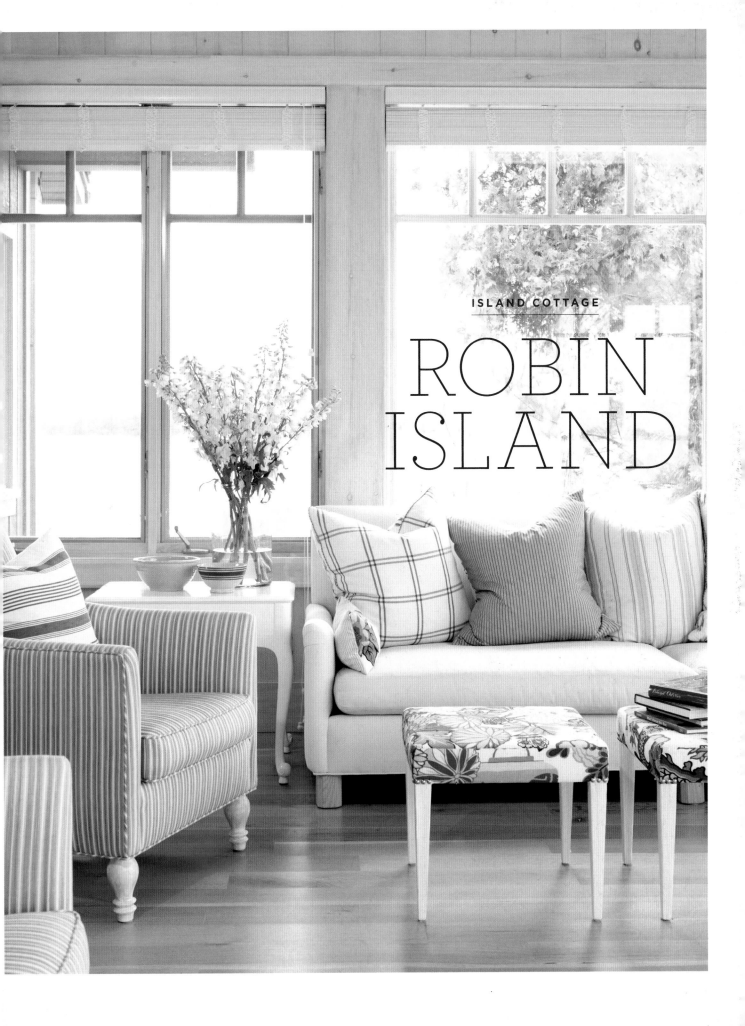

ISLAND COTTAGE

ROBIN ISLAND

FOLLOW THE WEATHER

We're on an island in the wide-open water of Georgian Bay, so we get some pretty awesome storms with winds ranging up to one hundred kilometres an hour! We'd always dreamed of having a "storm room," and this became the driving force of our expansion. In order to really be "in" the weather, you need lots of glass, so we opted for something that's more solarium in feel. With giant sliding doors and huge expanses of window, there's no escaping the marvels of Mother Nature.

LOUNGE LIZARD

We wanted every seat in the living
room to be oriented to the views
outside, so I paired chaises end to end
as the ultimate relaxation spots.
Forget the stuffy rules of furniture
arranging and do what makes
sense for how you live.

OPEN AND SHUT

When considering your window needs, it's important to factor in furniture placement. While I was drawn to the idea of having multiple doors leading outside, I found it limited the amount of seating I could squeeze into our sixteen-by-sixteen-foot space. If we had doors on all three sides, there would be no room for luxurious, deep, comfy seating, so I opted to put one giant pair of sliding doors on the south end and make the other two walls casement windows, which crank open wide and give the feeling of a screened porch on a hot day.

↑ DEFER
TO NATURE

In every project, I look to nature for inspiration. When selecting the exterior colours, I traipsed out to the farthest point on the island with paint chips in hand and tried to match the tones in the big granite boulders. When picking an exterior palette, make sure you have enough of a contrast so they read as two different colours from a distance. (I'm speaking from experience here, as the first colour I chose for the siding was far too close to the trim colour, and I had to reselect at the eleventh hour.)

→ HAVE AN ACCENT

I swoon for beautiful fabrics and patterns, but I often prefer them in small doses. When I find a dynamite print, I might only buy a couple of yards instead of upholstering large pieces with it. I like an unstructured and casual look that blends a variety of textures, prints, and colours. I'm not fussed about whether all the blues are the exact same shade, as I want a little variety. A touch of floral here with a hint of stripe there infuses that cool, relaxed mood of easy cottage living.

← GATHER ROUND

Relaxed lounge chairs with a William Birch arm profile float in a circular grouping of four between the kitchen and the dining areas, offering a spot to sit and chat while keeping out of the way of the action in the kitchen.

→ SPF FACTOR

An antique dresser makes a handy catch-all by the main door, and a vintage mirror surrounded by hooks hung with straw hats ensures no one heads out on a sunny day without proper cover. Elevate the simplest of everyday objects to functional art.

DOUBLE SIDED

In the "old days" our kitchen was cute and compact — and total chaos when cooking for a crowd. When my kitchen doubled in size by gobbling up the old dining area during the renovation, my first priority was to try to alleviate the bottleneck from the prep zones. I split the kitchen functions into two distinct areas, divided by the hallway that runs right through the kitchen space. Squatters, drinkers, and bakers to the left, please, and chefs to the right. The "fun" side of the kitchen combines the bar (with prep sink and bar fridge), an area designated for baking and non-cooking-related prep, and a counter-height seating area now dubbed the "lunch counter" (the perfect place for kids to snack and do arts and crafts). Two long runs in galley formation on the opposite side act as "mission control" and allow me to whip up my version of cottage gourmet without tripping over everyone else.

↘ WHAT YOU SEE

Just about every kitchen I design has an open display. I've been collecting vintage pressed glass, milk glass, and colourful ceramics for almost two decades and wanted to showcase them as functional art. But there's a truly practical argument for open display: if you can see where it came from, you know where to put it back once you've washed it!

↗ AT THE SHORE

We are surrounded by water, and I'm constantly looking for inspirational ways to embrace our surroundings. The fronts on the upper bar cabinets have seeded glass with delicate little bubbles reminiscent of the water after a wave has just crashed at the shore. This allusion to effervescence seemed doubly appropriate in the bar area, with all those fizzy drink options!

WATERY HUES

My love of watery palettes has become my signature in design. It's hard to pick which soothing, misty tones of muted blues, greens, and greys are my favourites, so I went with one of each and got not one, not two, but three shades of watery hues on my kitchen cabinets. Designing a new kitchen is your opportunity to get the details just right for you, so ask for what you want.

THE RIGHT DETAILS

The cabinetry is an extra-wide Shaker rail complemented by a tapered trim piece. Thanks to the magic of computers I was able to have a single initial monogram added to two of the lower cabinets for a touch of whimsy and fun.

↘ UP THE GOURMET ANTE

Bet you'd never guess by looking at it that my gourmet kitchen runs entirely off the grid, would you? Many assume green power means you need to sacrifice good looks, but thankfully that's not the reality. We've got a restaurant-worthy six-burner gas stove, two dishwashers, and a bar fridge to boot, all running off a combination of solar power and propane gas. As long as it's energy efficient, you can have all the conveniences of city power without the monthly bills!

GROCERIES

← BRING IN THE OLD

One struggle of designing a new cottage is creating a space that has soul and personality once completed. Antique corbels and painted wood panelling from an 1860s schoolhouse blend effortlessly with all the new elements. Adding mismatched stools, an old grocery sign, and all my vintage bits and bobs means that my cottage kitchen has all the charm of an old family cottage with the benefits of modern conveniences.

FAMILY-STYLE DINING

What's your chair preference? Some like a soft chair, others like plush, and some people (me!) like to snuggle up close to someone on a bench. Our dining table has something for everyone and is a study in mix and match. The common elements in all the seating options are an arched back, gently sweeping arm, and a lively mix of blue and green tones. By selecting a more varied seating arrangement, you may find your dining area becomes a more flexible and engaging place to gather.

LET THE VIEW BE THE STAR

One of my goals was to add a nod to more traditional cottage design with divided panes in the windows. It may not be a historic cottage, but that doesn't mean you can't borrow a few details, and nothing says brand-new cottage like giant panes of glass. If you want to maximize the views to the great outdoors, leave the bottom section of the windows as a full pane, and go for the Craftsman look of a band of small panes across the top.

KEEP IT REAL

When surrounded by rocks and trees, it's only right to keep your building materials in line. The most appropriate and best-looking materials are always the most natural. With a cedar roof, Douglas fir posts, and wood siding and soffits, the entire exterior has a rugged natural beauty created by installing the simplest of materials in a restrained yet elegant manner. The most pleasing details to the eye are often the ones that celebrate the installation over the design in an effort to blend architectural vision with the natural landscape.

→ THE RIGHT RED

Red, white, and blue is the epitome of summer style and adored by Alexander about as much as I love white, so I gave this summer scheme a shot in our bedroom. For me, the right shade is more tomato soup than cherry and more faded than fire truck. With fabrics that have a sun-washed intensity and a balance of cool denim blues and crisp whites, this room feels breezy and light.

← SATELLITE OFFICE

When duty calls and there's work to be done, you might as well make sure you can still enjoy the view. This desk was salvaged from a nearby university campus, and the sloped desktop is ideally suited to a bedroom as it makes it necessary to put away the pile of business papers when the workday is done.

WHAT LIES BENEATH

In our cottage, there's no need to worry about monsters hiding under the beds: there's no room for them! Since we are tight on space, a king-size bed frame with six giant drawers is a storage lifesaver.

Summer is a season for barefoot elegance, and nothing feels better underfoot than painted wood floors. They are easy to sweep up, glisten in the light, and allow the introduction of yet another summery hue to your design scheme. Sand between coats to remove any dust particles, and don't stop till you have a gleaming and beautiful finish (three coats is a good rule). As the promise of summer draws nearer, I can almost feel my bare feet gliding across those pretty painted floors.

↑ SHUTTER STYLE

Lining the hall to the tiny two-piece bath on the upper floor is a mirror image wall of floor-to-ceiling cabinets designed as his and hers wardrobes. More shipshape than walk-in, this compact combination of drawers and cabinets makes it remarkably easy to keep your wardrobe organized.

↗ MASTER CLASS

We created a private oasis with access off the master bedroom by taking advantage of the flat roof on top of the screened-in porch below. Tucked at the end of the long and narrow building, it feels like an upper deck on the prow of a ship.

↑ PLANT LIFE

The vanity had a former life as an outdoor garden table, and the handy little table beside the bathtub was a plant stand. With a bit of paint, these downtrodden treasures were brought to life with a new country look, and imagining their reuse is just part of the adventure.

↗ PEEKABOO

A transom window spans the width of the room, allowing you to see the sky while letting the breeze in but is just high enough that it prevents exposure to passersby on the deck and dock.

TACTILE TEXTURES

Rustic elements can be incorporated in many ways. Split-face mosaic on the wall behind the tub is both practical and decorative, while pebble mosaic on the shower floor provides a slip-proof surface (as well as a bonus foot massage), and accent bands of tumbled moonstone set in an otherwise simple shower stall punctuate the walls with yet another nod to natural materials.

GARDEN VARIETY

Cottage bedrooms offer a unique and refreshing take on style. Since they're only used in the warm summer months, there's no need to consider four-season comfort. With this in mind I decided to dial up the colour quotient and fill the bedrooms with perky prints evocative of a country wildflower garden. When it comes to island life, skip the neutrals and opt for bright delights.

QUILTING BEE

Perhaps I belonged to a quilting circle in a previous life, because something has to explain my deep affection for handmade quilts. You'll likely never find a pair that match, so focus instead on finding specimens with complementary colours and patterns and make the mix-and-match look part of the focus. Always be sure to inspect a vintage quilt before you buy it, and only buy pieces in good condition, or else you'll be starting up your own quilting bee to try to repair them.

To get the most authentic cottage look, we visited a handful of local dealers to source vintage treasures to furnish the rooms. Just about everything has been pre-loved. Quilts, lamps, dressers, side tables, desk, chairs, stools, textiles, and accessories all had previous lives before they made it to our island. The character and patina inherent in these pieces help bring a sense of history and charm to our new cottage. That they support the local merchants and cost a fraction of what it costs to buy new are just sprinkles on my sundae.

⌐ DESTINATION DREAMLAND

The cottage bunkie is a genius invention in my book. It's the ultimate getaway offering complete privacy and isolation and an easy solution for extra sleeping space. Struggling to keep within our allotted maximum floor space (as well as our maximum budget limits), the entire focus for our bunkie was to see how fast and how efficiently we could add a fabulous stand-alone cabin to our island. Since it's a summer-only property, the overall concept was about as simple as it gets: no heat, no running water, and no bells 'n' whistles.

← EXPAND YOUR HORIZONS

At eleven by fourteen feet, there's enough room for a queen-size bed with two side tables, a dresser, a small armchair with a side table, and a coat rack. When the sun is shining and the water beckons, what more do you need? Walls of windows can also make your space seem larger than it is by drawing the eye outside to the beautiful views.

← FAIRY-TALE SLUMBERS

There's more than one lesson to be learned from *The Princess and the Pea*. Thanks to the lofty perch offered by the four-poster bed, bunkie visitors can laze around and admire the magnificent view without even sitting up. Another advantage to the high bed is the space underneath — the perfect place for guests to stash their suitcases after unpacking.

ISLAND COTTAGE

BIRCH
POINT

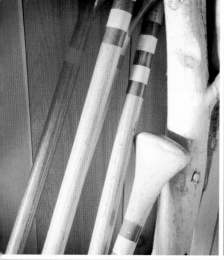

It was the first long weekend of summer, and we were out for a boat ride when we passed a dock with a For Sale sign on it. Alexander suggested we look at it. I figured that since we have a cottage, it would be of no interest, but his thinking was that they aren't making any more islands, and so a rental property is a sound investment. My colleagues at HGTV thought the adventure of turning a recreational property into an investment property would make entertaining TV, and before I knew it, we were documenting our DIY adventure of fixing up a remote 1950s island cottage on the open water of Georgian Bay before the sun set on summer.

↑ MODERN LOVE

The second we opened the door and saw the design of this cottage, complete with soaring ceilings, an original stone fireplace, and giant windows on three sides, it was clear this room had "good bones," but it felt drab and dated. With lots and lots of white paint, some new windows, and a rethink of the décor, the modern structure of the building clearly shines through, and 1950s design now looks way ahead of its time.

↑ ECO LIGHTING

Living off the grid calls for energy efficiency wherever possible. We use propane gas lights to illuminate the space at night. When your lights turn on with a match instead of by flipping a switch, it feels more rustic, and you become tuned in to your consumption levels, which is part of the adventure of island living.

↑ LIFE BY CANDLELIGHT

Believe it or not, our main source of light is candles!
If you love the look of a hanging candelabra but want
to be able to light and blow out the candles more easily,
you can hang a pulley from a hook in the ceiling and
attach a cord for easy raising and lowering of your
fixture. A cleat on the wall to hold it in place adds
a nautical nod.

↗ HIDE-A-BED

Cottage living is all about family and guests, so having
extra sleeping space is key. These built-ins were original
to the cottage and pull out to create two extra beds in
the living room. They were designed to take a standard-
size twin mattress that slides back into the backrest
when used as a sofa (so the seats aren't too deep), and
the ends that form the armrests are fitted with little
drawers for cards, games, and art supplies — talk about
clever design!

GO LOCAL

The local design movement doesn't get much closer than this! When thinking about an affordable dining-table base, I decided to look no farther than the surrounding woods. An old birch tree was growing in the middle of the main path and needed to be cut down, so I worked with our carpenter to turn it into a rustic dining-table base. The natural bark and curvy limbs are part of the casual charm, and you can't beat the price of do-it-yourself furniture.

← TREASURE HUNT

I scored these funky mid-century dining chairs at an antique store for just fifty dollars each. When shopping for vintage finds, you may need to see past the existing colour to find your diamond in the rough. These were originally orange and brown — and very retro — but feel fresh and fun repainted in a watery tone. The streamlined style of these chairs is a fitting tribute to the cottage's '50s heritage.

↑ FIRESIDE CHATS

With some inexpensive furniture finds and an easy, breezy mix of patterned fabrics, you can turn any room from passé to parfait. These cane chairs are wide and deep enough to be comfy fireside loungers, yet light enough to swing around and face the water views in the lounge area when the sun goes down. When planning a multifunctional room, flexibility is key.

STORAGE SCORE

Instead of a hidden corner cabinet that's tough to access, reorient the cabinet to face out into the adjoining space. These drawers now offer useful and easy-access storage for the breakfast bar and adjacent dining area.

TODAY'S
WEATHER

SUNNY
&
HOT!

Wear your
Sunscreen!

OPEN VIEWS

A wall with a pass-through separated
the kitchen from the living area. Since
the wall wasn't a structural element,
we took it down (and I helped with the
demolition!). This one small change
made a world of difference in the way
the main living space now functions.
If you're thinking about redesigning
your kitchen, start by investigating
what needs to stay and what's easy to
change — an open plan might be more
accessible than you thought!

ORIGINAL DETAILS

The cottage came with its original contents. Not everything was destined to stay once redesigned, but the original kitchen dishes blended seamlessly with the new décor scheme and were proudly displayed on the original shelves.

↑ GO NATURAL

Custom-fabricated counters are pricey and require two site visits (first to measure, then to install), but solid butcher block can be ordered online in lengths that can be cut to size on-site, saving both dollars and hassle.

↗ REMOTE ACCESS

When you're working in a remote location, easy solutions are needed. To allow maximum flexibility and minimum investment, I opted to use ready-to-go cabinetry (which could be configured on-site to create the best layout). Instead of applying the standard side gables and finishing panels, I applied tongue-in-groove pine panelling to the sides of the cabinets and on the underside of the island. It creates a fluid transition to the walls of the cottage and helps marry existing old elements with new ones.

→ TWO IS BETTER THAN ONE

If the cabinet door profile you are considering comes in more than one colour, try a mix-and-match approach. Watery blue uppers (with white knobs) and white lowers (with blue knobs) reflect the colours of clouds and sky and reinforce the cottage-casual vibe.

DO NOT DISTURB

Cottages are designed for gathering as a group and coming together, but sometimes a little space and privacy is needed. A painted lounge chair and a vintage rattan-seat grouping provides a spot for a quiet breakfast or peaceful escape with a summer read.

ORIGINAL CHARM

When we started, the interior walls were a number of different shades of natural wood. Painting and staining the wood unified the rooms and freshened them up so the colours and patterned fabrics could shine. Instead of painting it all out, the ceiling and rafters in the bedroom were left natural for a bit of warmth and to pay tribute to the original cottage. When modernizing an existing building, try to keep some elements that are a touchstone to the past.

← AT THE SHORE

I'm drawn to interiors that feel connected to their surroundings. I like to feel that there is a seamless flow between indoors and out, and one of the most effective ways to establish this connection is with colour. With windows on three sides, the main bedroom feels like a tree house, but the windows also run right to the floor, so it appears as though the water connects with the bedroom floor when you are standing in the room. Painted in a watery hue, it feels as if you could just wade right in.

↑ YOURS AND MINE

The original cottage was thoughtfully designed with plenty of built-in storage, so little additional furniture was needed. Tucked tight under the windowsills, these his and hers dressers offer ample storage for summer clothes while doubling as bedside tables. To spruce them up, the frames were painted white and the drawer fronts in a contrasting silvery grey, while the dated black tops were replaced with sleek stainless steel.

MINTY FRESH

Formerly dressed in a very retro scheme of banana yellow and glossy black, this little bathroom was ripe for a revamp. Instead of a costly custom vanity, a simple support for the marble countertop was made with rough lumber, then trimmed with a piece of pine across the apron. Vintage stainless baskets on slatted shelves make for easy-access extra storage. A vintage rattan mirror looks minty fresh thanks to a coat of pale green paint to tie into the marble counter, and glass shelves built into the wall help keep the counter surface clutter-free. Overall, a few little changes prove that making a dramatic difference doesn't always require a major renovation.

INSPIRATION STRIKES

Every room needs a jumping-off point. I found this amazing vintage blanket in the linen cupboard when we bought the cottage and embraced it as the colour scheme for the room. If you're looking to bring cottage style home, stick to simple, washable cotton fabrics that epitomize carefree elegance.

↑ GUEST ROOM

This guest room was created out of what used to be the storage room for cottage gear. Installing a wall to make the area two-thirds bedroom and one-third storage allowed us to gain a bedroom without giving up much-needed storage. Talk about value added!

↑ PATTERN PLAY

There's no rule that says your panelling needs to run vertically or horizontally. Installing wide pine boards in a chevron pattern creates interest on the wall and eliminates the need for a headboard.

← WHITEWASH IT

Love the grain of natural wood but not so keen on the yellowy tone of honeyed pine? Get out your brush and roller and apply some whitewash stain. The semitransparent stain will give your walls a light creamy wash, while letting the knots and wood grain shine through.

HANG TEN

Sometimes the best solution for art is simply to work with what you've got. These vintage skis came with the cottage and pay homage to the original use of the room as a storage facility, while the chevron pattern echoes the opposite wall.

When budget is the name of the game, you've got to work with what you've got. We placed the dividing wall to allow us to keep the existing sink and dressed it with simple finishing touches.

MAXIMUM EXPOSURE

Cottage living centres on spending as much time as possible in the great outdoors. But sometimes it doesn't seem so great if the bugs are buzzing about, hence the genius of a screen porch. The cottage was built with a cantilevered overhang from the upper level, which made enclosing the existing porch a breeze. A built-in bench with a flip-up lid provides storage for pillows when the inclement weather rolls in.

↑ CABIN CLASS

Reminiscent of a summer-camp cabin, the existing bunkroom had style and space-saving features in equal parts. The built-in bunks boast storage compartments and shelves. Clearly borrowed from the fundamentals of boat design, each one is like a snug little berth. With a maximum occupancy of five, this room celebrates the old adage of the more the merrier!

← SPLASH, DRY, REPEAT

Sunny days at the cottage involve a repetitive cycle of jumping in the lake, drying off, and doing it all again. You can try to get kids to put everything neatly in drawers, but it likely won't work. To keep soggy towels and bathing suits off the floor, I installed a row of galvanized dock cleats as hooks.

← TRUE BLUE

Pink is for girls and blue is for . . . everyone. When selecting a unisex palette that appeals to boys and girls both young and old, I don't think you can err with bold blues. A medley of graphic prints makes a one-size-fits-all scheme drawn from the beauty of lake and sky.

LIGHTS OUT

Originally built without any electricity, this cottage is the epitome of off-the-grid living. Now outfitted with solar power, each room has minimal lighting to help it retain the original rustic vibe, while still offering a few creature comforts. Taking a sympathetic approach to blending old with new, we outfitted the bunks with pulleys and buckets so the kids can stash their treasures and keep a flashlight close at hand for evening reads. It may seem odd to live a life without abundant available light, but what isn't taken for granted becomes that much more precious.

What lured us into buying this cottage was the original charm and character. The goal was to update on a budget a building that was more than sixty years old while maintaining the integrity of what was already there. Since budget was the key, we invested a healthy dose of sweat equity. Pitching in and getting involved in the transformation of your home is not only fun but rewarding. The pride of being able to say that you did it with your own two hands makes all the effort worthwhile.

OFF THE GRID ↘

Harnessing the sun to create your own energy is easier than you might think — plus it comes with the added benefit of never receiving a hydro bill. Alexander cleared a part of the woods and then designed and built the solar shed with the panels mounted on the roof and the mechanics that harness and convert the power hidden inside the shed. The south-sloping roof is designed and located to attract maximum sun rays and minimum shadows.

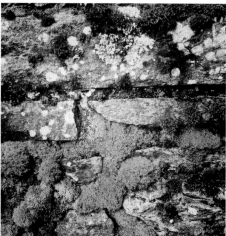

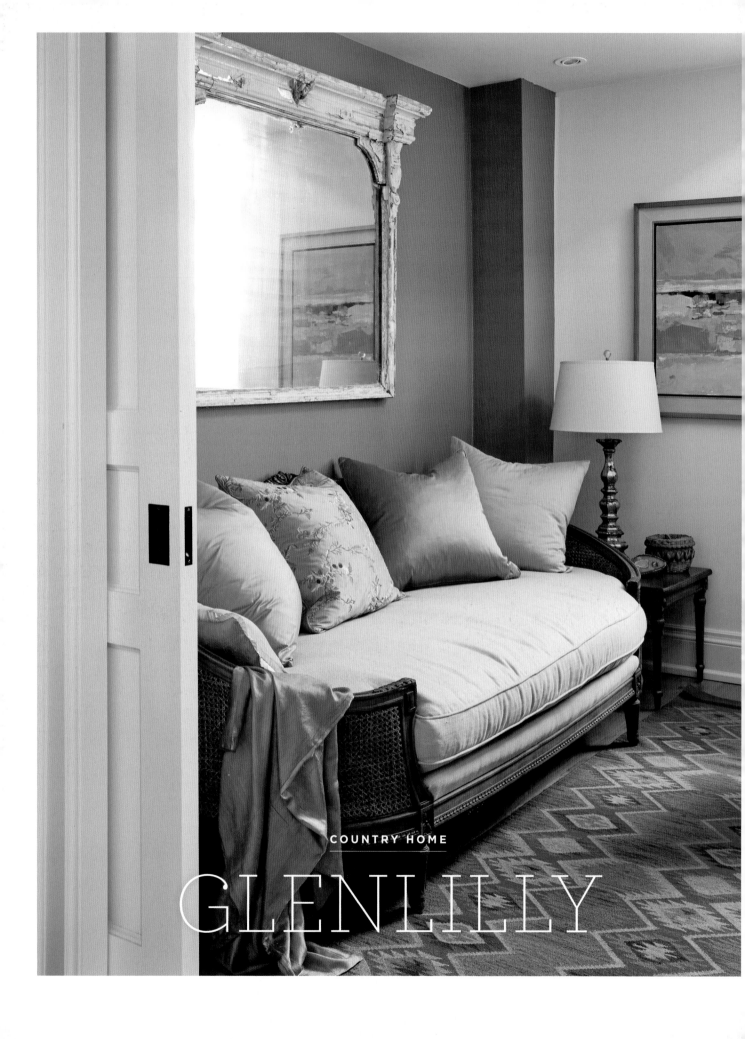

COUNTRY HOME

GLENLILLY

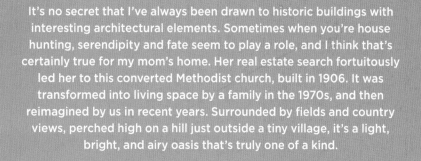

It's no secret that I've always been drawn to historic buildings with interesting architectural elements. Sometimes when you're house hunting, serendipity and fate seem to play a role, and I think that's certainly true for my mom's home. Her real estate search fortuitously led her to this converted Methodist church, built in 1906. It was transformed into living space by a family in the 1970s, and then reimagined by us in recent years. Surrounded by fields and country views, perched high on a hill just outside a tiny village, it's a light, bright, and airy oasis that's truly one of a kind.

OPEN KITCHEN

My mom's kitchen embraces all
the benefits of its open concept
and anchors the overall living space.
To accentuate the soaring ceilings,
we stacked a row of twenty-four-
inch cabinets above the main run
of uppers, creating drama and plenty
of storage so everything can be
tucked neatly away. If you like to
work as a team in the kitchen,
which we always do, start by
planning the island first, and
let the rest of the components
flow around.

RAISE THE ROOF ↑

Not many spaces have rooflines like a church, or the amazing height volumes that result from these lofty interiors, so I decided to play up the lean lines of the living/dining area with these tall and skinny vintage chairs. If you're dealing with spaces that connect from one to the next, you might want to try using light and airy pieces that allow you to enjoy the sight lines from one room to the next instead of blocking it with a wall of solid upholstery.

COUNTRY STYLE ↗

Whitewashed pine cupboards in a simple panelled design are well suited to the historic roots of the country structure. You can never go wrong with natural materials and restrained details.

→ BLUE SKIES

This sunroom is about as close as it gets to being outside. Since the church is built into a hill, I think this room is like being in the clouds, so I dressed it to feel as ethereal as the silver lining of any cloud might be. You can never go wrong by looking out the window and drawing inspiration from the vistas that surround you. If you're going to kick back and watch the clouds go by in your favourite room, might as well feel like you're living on a cloud, right?

↖ CLEAR AS DAY

It's never too early to start looking for lighting in the renovation process, as finding the right pieces can take time. My mom bought this Waterford chandelier from an estate sale while the interior of the church was still in demolition mode. I think all this sparkly loveliness served as motivation in her mind that one day the dust would be gone and everything would shine. And so it was.

→ OH, HONEY

At the beginning, the sunroom was all honey-stained and lacquered pine, which made it cozy, but once it was all painted, the focus changed from being in the room to looking through the room to what lies beyond.

I subscribe to the opinion that every home (and especially one in the country) is better with a wood-burning fireplace. Of course, one never existed in the original incarnation of this building, but thanks to modern innovations such as the wood-burning fireplace insert, you can easily add it during a renovation, then clad it to suit your style.

The upper level was reconfigured to create a master suite. To harness the best light and views from every vantage point, we opted for double doors into the bedroom and repurposed antique Egyptian window panels that now open onto the main space. The stair landing also makes a great stage for after-dinner entertainment when grandchildren come to visit!

← PRETTY AS A PICTURE

As a child, I loved tiptoeing into my mom's room, opening her closets, inhaling the scent of perfume, and admiring all the pretty things that filled the shelves and hangers. I especially loved playing with her jewellery and scarves, so this bedroom seems reminiscent of all the things I loved about where I grew up. With crystals that look like watery droplets, an etched Venetian mirror, and delicate touches throughout, this bedroom is tailored to the quiet elegance that surrounds my mom. When it comes to designing the most personal space in your home, let it be a true reflection of you and fill it with the things you love.

Crafting a home for contemporary living out of a former place of worship has its challenges. Since the church never had a second level, the bedroom is tucked up into the roofline. When you're trying to create a light-filled room from a space that isn't "all that," palette plays an important role. Sometimes all you need to give impact is the lightest wash or hint of colour. Instead of bold hues, think about the delicacy of a watercolour painting and opt for tints that speak in hushed tones — it's just what's needed for a restful retreat.

← ROOM WITH A VIEW

I crave flexibility in the way rooms
are used and want them to be
as multifunctional as possible.
Placing a table in front of a
window (or opening) allows you
to see everything from a different
perspective. This antique drop-leaf
table is a bold accent in an otherwise
subdued environment and makes
a simple yet useful writing desk.

SANDSWEPT ↗

It's impossible to go wrong
with a naturally neutral palette
in a bathroom. Classic, pure-white
elements paired with the soft
striations of a limestone floor
and chair-rail accent band create
a warm environment rooted
in a muted palette.

← THE RIGHT RATIO

Making a brand-new bathroom feel layered and authentically detailed is easier than you might think. By all means embrace the latest innovations in plumbing and fixtures, but then infuse the room with character through the addition of vintage and antique accents such as lighting, mirrors, and storage. It's a match made in heaven.

↙ VICTORIAN REVIVAL

There's no need to struggle with designing and then commissioning a custom vanity when you can convert an existing antique piece of furniture to be exactly what you need. The original character and charm are simply an added bonus, and in this case the original pine washstand came with a shaped gallery around the sides, which was removed to accommodate the marble top, then added back on. The little details of design inspire me, and this porcelain vessel sink was chosen as a nod to the ironstone bowl that would likely have sat atop this washstand originally.

As a child, I learned a lot about colour mixing from my mom. From fashion to home décor, she specialized in experimenting with and embracing unexpected combinations, often inspired by the palettes in her garden. Pink alone could be prissy, but when accented with chartreuse like the first leaves of spring and tempered with oyster greys, it makes this room feel both sophisticated and lively.

LOUNGE LUXE

The daybed in this lounge lets the room be used as extra sleeping quarters, if needed, and the antique Biedermeier chairs are sculptural accents with decorative presence that can easily be picked up and rearranged.

↓ COUNTRY STYLE

What makes country style appealing to me is the relaxed and effortless mix-and-match ease of casual living. You don't need to overthink your mix of textiles; just play with pattern, like a patchwork quilt that stitches together a variety of elements to create a unified whole.

↓ FLEA MARKET FIND

If you're looking for high-quality lighting at bargain prices, be on the lookout for vintage alabaster lamp bases at flea markets and consignment shops. I'm often amazed that I can buy carved solid stone for what a basic new lamp might cost, so I always snap them up.

↑ WAKE-UP CALL

If you're away from the buzz of the city, one of
the most prominent sounds is the birds singing in
the trees. From early morning they happily chirp
away. For the kids' guest room, I couldn't resist
using a reissued document-print fabric that hung
in a young girl's bedroom at a historic garden estate
in Rhode Island.

← DON'T BE SO SERIOUS

In my rule book for pattern mixing, nothing should ever
be too predictable. The bird is sophisticated and classic,
so it needs to be lightened up by more playful elements
such as the oversize apricot polka dot, cheerful banded
bedding, and a bold, floral hooked rug.

← ACCENTUATE THE DETAILS

An Eastlake-style pedestal table with chip-carving
details makes a pretty shared bedside table thanks
to the lyrical lines and whimsical flourishes that
define the style.

← KEEP THE CHARM

You can easily transform the look of inexpensive flea
market finds — such as these vintage and antique
furnishings — from traditional to country fresh with
a shiny coat of paint.

PAISLEY ACRES

I'm a born and bred city girl, but that all changed seven lucky years ago. We'd been dreaming about fixing up a farmhouse and spent weekends combing the country roads in search of a diamond in the rough just begging for a polish. A local real estate agent tipped us off to a century-old brick house with views out over a charming orchard filled with historic apple and pear trees and surrounded by fifty acres of rolling farmland. Thrilled, we bought the farm and set about transforming it from forlorn to family-friendly for my HGTV series *Sarah's House*. It didn't take long for us all to become smitten with the pleasures of life in a quaint rural town, and despite moving on to a new property, we're frequent visitors to the cozy country home that turned us from city slickers to weekend farmers.

← APPLE INSPIRED

There are four sets of double closet doors in the mudroom plus a door for the powder room, which totals nine doors. When I thought about the sports gear and garden tools that would constantly be tossed into these closets, I worried about how they'd show chips, scratches, and fingerprints if painted white. One glance out the windows to the orchard and I knew they had to be painted a brilliant apple red. A farmhouse shouldn't be serious or pretentious, and a bright and cheery hello in the mudroom extends a proper country welcome.

↖ LEAVE ROOM

Instead of installing wall-to-wall storage cabinets on every available inch of the room, I opted to leave space for freestanding furniture. The pine buffet and dry sink both give unique flavour to the room thanks to their patina and authentic character. Mix equal parts old and new for a recipe that will deliver on both storage and style.

← PRACTICALLY PANELLED

Nothing says country charm like tongue-in-groove panelling. It's not just pretty, it's also incredibly practical. In a high-traffic area, drywall can easily get chipped and banged, but stained pine develops a patina as it ages, looking more chic than shabby. While you're at it, why not extend the panelling onto the ceiling and run it in a different direction and in a slightly different colour to add interest!

→ GO RETRO
OVER REPRO

Today's kitchens often feature architectural details that are reproduced to create a look of grandeur. Instead of getting new pieces that look old, I went for the real deal with vintage corbels (to support a shelf and the vent hood), newel posts (to create legs for the island and to replicate an old stair detail), hardware, and lighting. You may find old pieces with a story to tell for less than you'd pay for new — plus hunting in salvage shops is the best kind of treasure hunt!

← REMEMBER WHAT
YOU LOVED

If you've bought an old home, you were likely drawn to some of the original features. Try to remember your affection for authentic details once the renovation gets under way. I was adamant about restoring and refinishing the original wood floors throughout the house despite continual recommendations that it would be easier to rip them out and put in something new. I admit they're not perfect — they've got gaps and are uneven — but the rustic, original floor with marks, stains, and telltale signs of wear and tear makes the house feel rooted in history.

I find the look of pot lights at odds with traditional style, so I tried to use as few as possible. If you place junction boxes carefully to highlight work areas, you'll find you have all the task lighting you need. Instead of a ceiling punctuated with pots, you can achieve a rustic and romantic flair by mixing and matching vintage fixtures. (For this country-casual look, I've combined galvanized French industrial shades and brass-toned mercury glass.)

↑ EMBRACE THE ECCENTRIC

Standard counter height is thirty-six inches above the floor, but that's not always possible. The original window openings had a sill height of only thirty inches, so instead of reconfiguring two of the kitchen windows, I installed two sections with lowered counters. You may never experience this design feature in your own kitchen, but I found lowered counters make unloading groceries easy, and they help minimize the look of clutter from items sitting on the counter. Bonus: they provide the perfect perch!

↑ LOOK FOR A SIGN

I'm forever on the lookout for fun elements to bring a bit of old-school whimsy to my designs. The first purchase I made for the farmhouse was a vintage sign that announces LUNCH SERVED TO-DAY. I bought this as motivation to remind me that one day the project would be complete and lunch could indeed be served, as well as so much more. This little table with plush cane chairs was in constant use for everything from early-morning coffee to late-night chats. Never underestimate the importance of a comfy spot in the hub of your home.

← STEP IT UP

When I lived in a loft apartment in my twenties with a girlfriend, I decorated our stairs with vintage house numbers and a colourful paint runner. Nearly two decades later I repeated myself and spent the better part of a weekend transforming this simple country staircase from plain to playful. You're never too old to have a sense of humour, and a little DIY is always good for the creative soul.

Soaring high ceilings add drama, volume, and wow to a room, but you don't need cathedral proportions to get the effect. If you go too high, it will dwarf all the furnishings and make it a veritable feat to create a feeling of intimacy and warmth (not to mention amp up your utility bills with all the heat that gets stuck up in the peak). This ceiling is fourteen feet at its highest point, and that more than does the trick.

↑ HEART AND SOUL

The heart of a country home is the hearth, and this one can be seen all the way from the mudroom entry, so getting the details right was a high priority. For the mantel, pale limestone blocks were installed with a section of salvaged bay window trim from a historic building, while an antique bank crest makes for an innovative art alternative on the wall above.

↑ BRING THE FIELDS IN

I was craving a bit of outside influence on the walls, and the hay in the fields nearby is so beautiful when it shimmers in the afternoon light that I decided to harness that lustre. Pale and silvery grasscloth lends textural richness to the walls above the chunky chair rail, while a rich orange clay tone gives a powerful boost to the lower wall section.

→ AUTUMNAL HUES

Those of us who live
in an area that
experiences the four
seasons know the all-
too-brief and fleeting
beauty of their turning
colours. In an effort to
celebrate the joys of my
most favourite season
(while also drawing
out the colours in the
antique Sarouk Persian
carpet), the pillows on
the upholstery are drawn
from the harvest-inspired
shades of the turning
leaves and executed in
a dynamic mix of velvet,
wool, and silk.

← FRAME THE VIEW

A country setting doesn't
necessitate drapes for
privacy, but I can't live
without them. On chilly
evenings, closed drapes
brighten the room and
diminish the stark look of
black windows, and big
rooms with large volumes
can benefit from tactile
touches. Simple yet
elegant drapes will also
soften and frame your
view to outside.

Instead of a suite of furniture, I prefer the casual, eclectic look of a collection of pieces from different sources. An antique pine cabinet housing fine china and crystal, an 1890s walnut dining table that can extend eleven feet to accommodate a crowd, and comfortable rattan armchairs reinforce our laid-back approach to entertaining at home. When designing a dining room, the key is to create an environment that you want to spend time in, so choose what works for your entertaining style.

LOOKING BACK

To embrace the boundary between old house and new addition,
the original exterior brick wall was left exposed. The rich cast
of the red brick served as inspiration for the russet tone used throughout
the dining room. Whenever possible, it makes good design sense
to celebrate the authentic details of the building you're working with
instead of burying their charm and character by building over them.

→ FAMILY STYLE

The original dining room featured a single window that became the archway leading to the addition during the renovation, but the entire south-facing wall was solid brick. The renovation introduced an oversize window bump with a deep window seat to make the room brighter and bigger looking. I grew up at a family cottage that featured long benches beneath the windows where little kids could curl up and doze off while listening to the adults talking at the table, and our girls spent many weekend evenings climbing onto the window bench, drawing the drapes, and repeating history. Whimsical Victorian house brackets with a fanciful flower motif were stripped to reveal layers of original paint, then hung in the archway that connects the dining room to the kitchen.

→ SUITE RETREAT

There are many takes on the ultimate spot for the master retreat, and there's no one right answer in design or architecture. It all comes down to personal preference, lifestyle, and planning. When thinking about a house filled with guests and family, we opted for a ground-floor location, removed from the hustle and bustle of the gathering rooms in the house, and in a location surrounded by the natural landscape.

→ BREAK OUT

The beginning of this bedroom scheme was an antique quilt in the most unusual colour combination found at a flea market. Everyone has his or her shopping weaknesses, and textiles have always been one of mine. Marigold yellow and pumpkin orange haven't been known to be my favourite colours, but I believe you should embrace the opportunity to experiment whenever possible.

→ TWO FOR ONE

Over-scaled prints are a recurring element in my interiors. Once it was rolled off the bolt, I noticed this floral print features four distinct blooms within the overall pattern, so I chose to centre one of the four flowers on each seat and back, resulting in a his and hers combination that makes a unique and distinct pair.

← ROUGH IT UP

Every room in the house is panelled, wainscotted, chair-railed, and detailed with some traditional country-themed wood detail. I experimented with a variety of patterns and applications to give each room its own flair, so to contrast the fine antiques and high vertical proportions in this room, I installed rough-sawn panelling horizontally to play up the rustic setting, then stained it in an opaque oyster tone to add a cooling element to all the fiery colours in the fabrics.

→ FIRE UP A FANTASY

Building a new structure is synonymous with freedom. It's your chance to get what you want and prioritize the details that matter most to you. In every project I subscribe to a save-and-splurge approach to prioritization that helps me get what I want without feeling that I sacrificed to get it. Knowing that a wood-burning fireplace would be a splurge, I pulled back the reins and selected a more rustic grade of cherry for the floors (shorter boards and more knotholes add more character and are barely noticeable once covered with a rug).

↙ TREASURE TROVE

It all started with a tattered chenille bedspread that I found in the upstairs closet. The centre of the bedspread was threadbare from use, but the perimeter was preserved, so I snipped the salvageable sections to turn into a bed skirt and accent pillows. They just don't make chenille coverlets like they used to, and there's nothing softer or more appropriate for the country!

← PRETTY IN PINK

A deep aubergine floral with a lyrical pattern provides a rich burst of colour on the drapery and headboard. The peaked shape of the headboard echoes the slope of the ceiling with a cutout detail that was inspired by a Georgian-style door pediment. Mixed with polka dots and stripes, the room is designed to be more exuberant than elegant, befitting of a young girl.

← TABLE TALK

Even little ones need surfaces beside their bed to store their treasures and worldly belongings. But a matched pair is not mandatory. If you focus on choosing one piece for storage and one to serve as a table, desk, or vanity, you can add features that consume less space. My nature is to paint everything, but I found the extra-dark mahogany tone of these two items perfectly pulled out the deepest shade of the stem in the floral fabric.

↗ WOODLAND DELIGHT

Lighting isn't just practical; it adds huge decorative impact to every room, especially when you've got high ceilings that draw the eye up. This vintage French enamel pendant is pretty yet not prissy and appears wrapped in delicate woodland wildflowers.

← DAYDREAMING

The long proportions of the shared family bathroom necessitated a narrow tub profile. This volcanic limestone bathtub has an elegant form with a dramatically raised profile at one end that's placed so it's ideally suited to leisurely soaks while gazing out the window and watching the clouds roll by.

← PREP SCHOOL

Cotton plaid drapes in a preppy palette reminiscent of a blue oxford-cloth button-down and khaki pants channel a country picnic. The contrast of beige and white on the trellis-patterned floor is repeated in the panel detail on the walls, then accented with breezy blue on the surrounding walls.

→ VINTAGE VANITY

The vanities are crafted from a matched pair of vintage pine dressers and had their original wood tops replaced with creamy honed marble. When converting a dresser to a vanity, you can preserve the utility of the drawers by notching out a channel for the drain while still maintaining most of the storage space. A bonus is that the space between the two allows enough room for hanging towel storage.

CHECK IN

You may wind up feeling like Goldilocks, but you really should sleep in every bed in your home to assess what works and what doesn't. Is the lighting adequate for reading? Is there enough space to put away clothes and necessities? Is the bed comfortable? Are the pillows good, or did you wake up needing a chiropractor? Do the drapes block out the early-morning rays? If you don't know the answer to these questions, you may want to check in to your own guest room and experience it first-hand. This room was the top choice of every guest who ever stayed with us, so I know it was done right.

→ COUNTRY SLUMBERS

Far away from all-night sirens and the hum of the city, country slumbers are inspired by fresh breezes and chirping crickets, so what better place to seek inspiration than the rolling countryside? Since most of the house is a cornucopia of colour, this guest room takes a break and references the subtler tones of a stormy sky in smoky blues and earthy neutrals. No matter what the weather, there's inspiration just beyond the windowsill!

→ DIVIDE AND CONQUER

Sloped ceilings often lead to pondering where to apply paint and how to deal with the tricky condition presented by the lack of right angles. Do you wrap the colour up and over? Do you paint the end walls in one colour and the rest in a second colour? By installing a piece of chair-rail trim at the top of the vertical wall, just beneath the slope, a crisp delineation is created between walls and ceiling, allowing you to paint the room in two distinct tones — and I'm always in favour of the "more is more" approach to paint colours.

PASS ON PROVENANCE

The perfect vanity for your bathroom doesn't necessarily have a glamourous past. This one was originally a tool cabinet and came complete with years of grime, dirt, and some vintage machine tags. It just happened to be the right height, depth, and size for my needs (not more than thirty-six inches high and twenty to twenty-two inches deep is a good standard), and the bargain price made the scrubbing down worthwhile. If budget is on the agenda for your bath renovation, opt for a countertop that's just three-quarters of an inch thick. I find a simple bevelled-edge profile looks better and is less chunky than the go-to standard of one and a half inches that requires doubling up the edge.

BIRDS AND BEES

I've long been a fan of botanical engravings, and this fabric buzzing with bees and blooming with country-road flowers feels crisp and modern in sunny citrus yellow. Reinforce your fabric choice by painting the outside of your old enamelled bathtub — and even the mirror frame — in a matching hue for an instant pick-me-up!

→ ORCHARD VIEWS

This north-facing guest room looks out onto the apple orchard, cornfields, and the lake on the horizon, offering all the inspiration necessary for a country-chic colour palette of crisp apple red, soft ochre yellow, and cool watery blue.

← CLOSET TALK

Standard, built-in closets can be considered a necessity for rooms that get daily use, but when guests aren't unpacking steamer trunks of garments, a simple solution suffices. I combined built-in drawers and cabinets with an open centre nook to create a daybed–cum–extra-sleeping-space.

← PERK UP

Give an old Victorian chair a New Age vibe and paint the frame in a bold colour for an unexpected accent of your signature shade.

A formal red-ground paisley pattern becomes more laid-back when juxtaposed with perky polka dots, rustic embroidered crewel, and charming ticking stripes. When you combine a variety of different patterns, the colours don't need to match exactly — that's the laid-back charm of country décor!

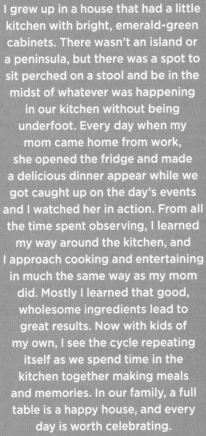

I grew up in a house that had a little kitchen with bright, emerald-green cabinets. There wasn't an island or a peninsula, but there was a spot to sit perched on a stool and be in the midst of whatever was happening in our kitchen without being underfoot. Every day when my mom came home from work, she opened the fridge and made a delicious dinner appear while we got caught up on the day's events and I watched her in action. From all the time spent observing, I learned my way around the kitchen, and I approach cooking and entertaining in much the same way as my mom did. Mostly I learned that good, wholesome ingredients lead to great results. Now with kids of my own, I see the cycle repeating itself as we spend time in the kitchen together making meals and memories. In our family, a full table is a happy house, and every day is worth celebrating.

IN OUR KITCHEN

SPRING & SUMMER

FIONA'S ALMOST-GUILT-FREE BANANA CHOCOLATE CHIP MUFFINS

These petite treats are so easy to make that Fiona has been whipping them up since she was a toddler. They are wholesome and delicious, with a hint of sweetness provided by the chocolate chips. Bake up a batch, pile them on a pedestal, and watch them disappear. One is never enough!

3	ripe or very ripe bananas
1/4 cup	salted butter
1/4 cup	demerara sugar or cane sugar
1 cup	organic yogurt
3	large eggs
2 tsp	vanilla extract
1 tsp	salt
1 tsp	baking soda
1 cup	unsweetened coconut flakes
2 cups	Flour Power Blend (see recipe below)
1 cup	dark chocolate chips
2 tbsp	extra-virgin olive oil

1 Preheat oven to 350°F.

2 In a food processor, combine bananas, butter, and brown sugar and purée until whipped smooth. Add yogurt, eggs, and vanilla and purée again until blended.

3 In a large bowl, combine salt, baking soda, coconut, and flour and stir together.

4 Pour the banana mixture into the dry mixture and stir with a spatula until just mixed. Do not overmix.

5 Pour in chocolate chips and fold them in until just combined.

6 Spoon the batter into mini-muffin tins. (I like to use silicone trays and brush olive oil into the base of the cups, then spoon about 1 heaping tablespoon into each cup.) Bake for 18 to 22 minutes.

MAKES 3 DOZEN

Note: If you want to omit coconut, you can substitute flour.

FLOUR POWER BLEND

Most of us are trying to make sure that what we put into our bodies is as healthy and nutritious as possible. I'm by no means a health nut, but I do strive to fill my diet with wholesome choices. In an effort to bolster comfort-food indulgences (think pancakes, waffles, and baked goods) with less processed flour and more nutrition, I started experimenting with alternatives to all-purpose flour. I now use this blend for most of my recipes in place of all-purpose flour. If you want to avoid gluten altogether, you can swap the dark rye flour out for quinoa flour. I keep this mix in a big glass canister so I can just scoop it out whenever I need it. If you're looking for the ingredients in your grocery store, check the health food section. The almond meal gives a slightly nutty flavour to recipes, while the flax makes it light and airy. This blend is kid-tested too!

Equal parts	dark rye flour	Mix all the ingredients together to ensure they are well blended, and store in an airtight canister or container.
	ground flax	
	ground almond meal	

GOOD START GRANOLA

A friend of ours runs a fabulous bakery in Old Montreal, and she shared this recipe with me more than a decade ago. Over the years I've altered it slightly, but the result is always the same — a delicious and nutritious way to get any day off to a good start!

8 - 10 cups	rolled oats (not quick cooking and preferably organic)
1 cup	slivered or sliced almonds
1 1/2 cups	unsweetened, desiccated coconut
1 1/2 cups	flaxseeds
1 cup	whole raw almonds
1 1/2 cups	pumpkin seeds (shelled, not salted or roasted)
1 1/2 cups	sunflower seeds (shelled, not salted or roasted)
1 cup	honey
1 cup	maple syrup
1 tsp	salt
2 tbsp	vanilla
1 cup	currants (or any other dried fruit)
1	banana (sliced)

1 Preheat the oven to 275°F. Mix the oats, slivered almonds, coconut, flaxseeds, whole almonds, pumpkin seeds, and sunflower seeds together in a big mixing bowl.

2 Pour the honey and maple syrup into a measuring cup. Add the salt, then pour in the vanilla (it liquefies the honey and makes it easy to stir in with the dry ingredients).

3 Drizzle the wet mixture over the dry ingredients (you may find it easier to split this into two mixing bowls, which I often do). Stir to coat the dry ingredients.

4 Once the dry ingredients are thoroughly coated, pour them out onto two large rimmed baking sheets and bake for 30 minutes. Remove from the oven, carefully stir to ensure the mixture on the bottom doesn't burn, and bake for another 30 minutes or until it's browned. Don't overbake, and don't try to cook at a higher temperature or it may burn.

5 Once cooled, stir in the currants and store in an airtight container.

6 Serve with plain organic yogurt, sliced banana, or fresh fruit, and drizzle with honey.

MAKES 12 CUPS

NIK'S MONTE CRISTO

In the early days of my TV career, I worked behind the scenes as a prop stylist and set decorator. One of the shows I worked on, called *Savoir Faire*, was all about entertaining, and that's where the host, Nik Manojlovich, introduced me to the Monte Cristo. I'm pretty sure you'll be glad I introduced you to it too!

2 slices	challah (egg bread)
2 tsp	mayonnaise
1/4 cup	roughly grated Gruyère (or other Swiss cheese)
3 slices	roasted turkey
1	egg
1 tbsp	milk (optional)
1 tbsp	butter
1 tbsp	whole-grain Dijon mustard
2 tbsp	pure maple syrup

1 Spread the inside of each slice of challah with a bit of mayonnaise. Place half the grated cheese on the bottom slice, followed by the turkey, the remainder of the cheese, and the second slice of bread.

2 Crack the egg into a wide, shallow bowl, add the milk, if using, and whisk until well blended.

3 Dip the bottom of the sandwich into the egg mixture and allow it to absorb the egg, then flip it over and dip the top side.

4 Melt the butter in a frying pan over medium heat. Place the sandwich in the pan and grill it for a few minutes on each side until golden brown.

5 The sandwich is done once the cheese is melted on both sides. If you are making these for a group, you might want to lightly grill them first, then transfer them to a preheated 350°F oven to continue to melt (and keep warm) for 5 to 10 minutes. Serve with mustard and syrup.

MAKES 1 SANDWICH

BANANA BLUEBERRY PANCAKES

Weekend breakfasts in our house usually involve three key ingredients: blueberries, maple syrup, and a frying pan. In an effort to sneak some extra nutrition into the kids, I transformed the standard pancake recipe into something more nutritious but just as delicious. Thanks to extra eggs, yogurt, hidden bananas, and juicy blueberries, these griddle cakes are great starter fuel for all weekend adventures. To make the batter extra light and fluffy, I prepare it in a blender. Just toss in the ingredients, and breakfast will be on the table in no time!

3	bananas
4	large eggs
1 cup	plain yogurt
1 cup	milk
2 tsp	vanilla extract
1 tbsp	baking powder
1/2 tsp	salt
2 cups	flour (you can use all-purpose flour or the Flour Power Blend on pg 205, or a mix of 1 cup quinoa flour and 1 cup all-purpose flour)
1 cup	blueberries (fresh or frozen)
	butter, for the frying pan
	maple syrup, for serving

1 In a blender or food processor, purée the bananas and eggs. Add the yogurt, milk, and vanilla and blend again.

2 In a mixing bowl, combine the baking powder, salt, and flour(s) and stir until combined.

3 Pour the wet mixture into the dry ingredients and mix lightly until just combined. Do not overmix.

4 Fold in the blueberries.

5 Preheat the oven to 275°F. Melt a pat of butter in a frying pan over medium heat. As soon as the butter starts to bubble, pour in the batter to make pancakes about 5 inches in diameter.

6 Once bubbles rise to the surface of the pancake, flip gently and cook the reverse side, 3 to 4 minutes per side depending on the heat of your stovetop.

7 Transfer the cooked pancakes to an oven-safe platter and keep them warm in the oven.

8 Repeat until the batter is used up.

9 Heat maple syrup for about 30 seconds in the microwave and pour it over the pancakes when served. Garnish with fresh blueberries (or cut peaches if desired).

MAKES ABOUT 12 PANCAKES

SUSU'S STRAWBERRY JAM

I remember picking strawberries in the fields near the cottage, then enjoying the sweet aromas that filled the cottage kitchen as my mom turned them into delicious jam. My mom skips the pectin and minimizes the sugar, so the jam is as pure and simple as possible.

2 quarts	fresh ripe strawberries (or you can use frozen berries)
3 tbsp	brown, demerara, or cane sugar, plus more if needed
1 tsp	butter

1 In a large saucepan with a heavy bottom (to prevent burning), gently stir the berries and sugar together without smashing the fruit. Let it sit for 10 minutes to allow the sugar to sink into the fruit. Add the butter.

2 Bring the jam to a gentle boil over medium heat (watch that it doesn't burn). Taste-test for sugar quantity. You can add a bit more if desired (which may be needed if the berries you are using don't have enough natural sugar).

3 Cook for 8 to 10 minutes, until the berries slump slightly. Stir gently but don't overmix or overcook, as the goal is to keep the berries mostly intact. If using frozen berries, cook the berries from frozen for about 20 minutes.

4 Allow the jam to cool in the pot, then let it stand at room temperature, uncovered, overnight to reduce the liquid.

5 Divide the jam into jars and keep refrigerated. Store any extra in the freezer for up to 1 year.

MAKES ABOUT 4 CUPS OF JAM

CONQUER THE WORLD JUICE

We all have those days when we feel we could use a boost or we just don't have time for a proper midday meal. When that happens to me, I turn to a tall glass of liquid goodness to get me through and power me up. Brimming with superfoods such as spinach and kale, and with lots of citrus zing, this juice is equal parts energizing, cleansing, and refreshing. Drink up!

2	apples, cored (with skin on)
2	lemons, peel cut off
1	lime, peel cut off
6	kale leaves, stems removed
3 sprigs	parsley
10	romaine leaves
1 inch	fresh ginger, peel removed
6-inch	piece English cucumber, peeled
1 cup	spinach

1 Using an electric juicer, process all the ingredients through the machine to extract the juice.

2 Stir, split between two glasses, and serve (or keep in an airtight container in the fridge for up to 2 days).

MAKES TWO 8-OUNCE GLASSES

BLT SALAD

A BLT sandwich is a perennial hit, but I've devised a way to enjoy all the salty crunch and refreshing snap of an old classic without the carb guilt. I like to serve it up on a big flat platter as a simple lunchtime salad. There are never any leftovers!

SALAD

12 slices	high-quality bacon
1 head	romaine lettuce
1	avocado
3/4 cup	grape tomatoes

DRESSING

1/2 cup	extra-virgin olive oil
3 tbsp	balsamic vinegar
1 tbsp	whole-grain Dijon mustard
	freshly ground sea salt and pepper

1 Cook the bacon until crispy, then set aside.

2 Make the salad: Wash and dry the romaine. Tear off whole leaves. Lay them in the bottom of a shallow bowl or on a platter.

3 Pit and peel the avocado and slice into thin wedges. Cut the tomatoes lengthwise. Place vegetables in a mound at the base of the platter.

4 Make the dressing: Combine the oil, vinegar, mustard, and salt and pepper to taste in a small bowl or pitcher. Drizzle the dressing over the salad without tossing it so that the presentation remains intact.

SERVES 4

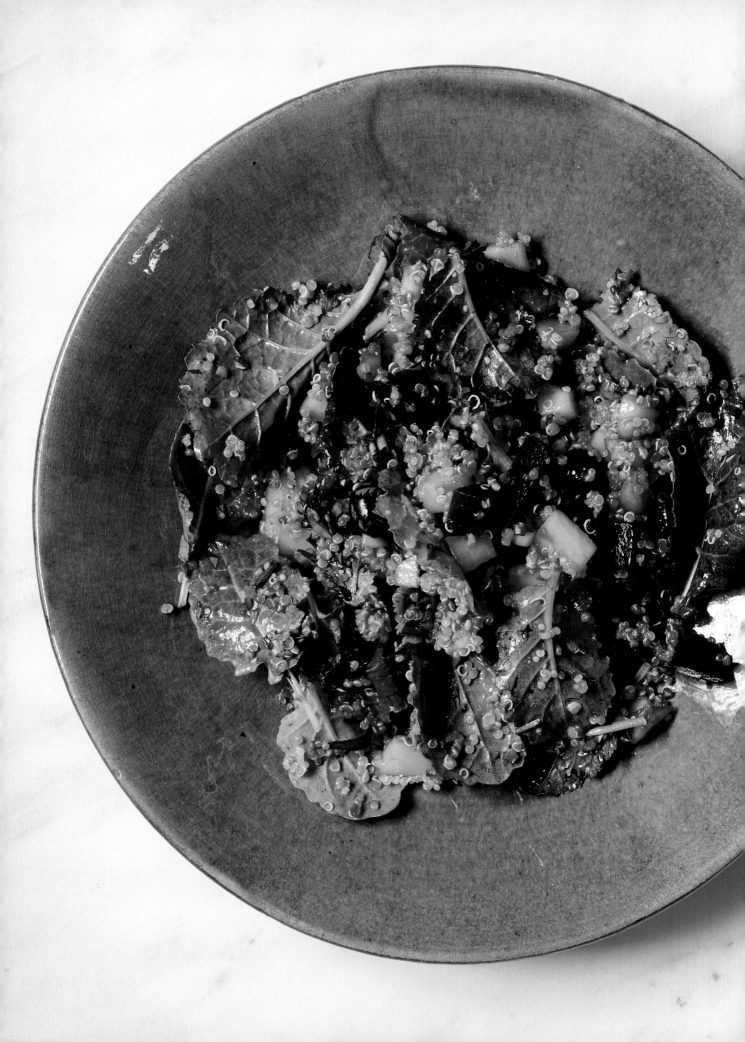

QUINOA, BEET, AND BABY KALE SALAD

Summers at the cottage are for impromptu get-togethers, which means fresh and fast meals. My friend and cottage neighbour Martha first shared her quinoa salad with me a few years ago, and I've been making a variation of it ever since. Quinoa is a superfood staple to keep in the pantry, while kale lasts well in the fridge, which makes this a dish ideally suited to island life. Of course, you don't have to have an island to enjoy it; you just have to like the idea of a healthy lifestyle!

SALAD

3	medium-size beets
1 cup	uncooked quinoa
3 – 4 cups	baby kale
1	avocado
1	mango
3	green onions
1/4 cup	fresh cilantro
1/2 cup	fresh basil
1/3 cup	fresh blueberries

DRESSING

	juice of one lime or lemon
1/3 cup	olive oil
2 – 3 tbsp	white balsamic vinegar
1 tbsp	whole-grain Dijon mustard
1 tbsp	honey
	freshly ground sea salt and pepper

1 Chop the stems off the beets. Place beets in a saucepan and cover with water. Bring to a boil, cover, and simmer for about 25 minutes (or until a sharp paring knife slides easily into the flesh). Rinse with cold water as soon as the beets are cooked, then drain and set aside. Once the beets are fully cooled, peel with a paring knife and cut into small chunks.

2 Prepare the quinoa according to the package directions. It will likely call for 2 cups water for 1 cup quinoa, but the result is better if you use 1 1/4 cups water. Set the quinoa aside and allow it to cool.

3 After the quinoa has cooked, put the kale in a large salad bowl and pour the cooled quinoa on top. You can use regular kale or baby kale, but I find the leaves are more delicate and less fibrous with baby kale.

4 Peel and dice the avocado. (It's better if the avocado is just ripe, but not too soft.) Add to the salad bowl along with the beets.

5 Peel the mango, then use a large knife to cut the fruit off the stone or slice the halves away from the stone, score the flesh, flip it inside out, and cut it away from the skin. Chop it into bite-size chunks. Add to the salad bowl.

6 Chop the white and light-green parts of the green onions, roughly chop the cilantro and basil, and add all to the salad bowl along with the blueberries.

7 Make the dressing: Combine the lime or lemon juice, oil, vinegar, mustard, and honey. Stir well (or shake in a lidded jar).

8 Pour three-quarters of the dressing on the salad and allow it to soak in (about 10 minutes). Save the remaining dressing to add before serving. Season to taste with freshly ground sea salt and pepper.

SERVES 6

GOLDEN BEET AND MINT SALAD

Beets are a superfood: they're energy boosters packed with lots of vitamins, act as kidney cleansers, and are heart healthy, but they are also just plain delicious. My neighbour owns a chain of Italian restaurants that I've been going to for twenty years. While beets and basil are a common duo, his restaurant menu pairs beets with mint. That was the inspiration for this salad. The mint is fresh, the arugula is spicy, the peas are crunchy, and the golden beets are pure summery heaven.

SALAD

3	medium-size golden beets
3/4 cup	arugula
3/4 cup	shelled fresh peas
10 leaves	fresh mint, roughly chopped

DRESSING

2 tbsp	balsamic vinegar
2 tbsp	freshly squeezed lemon juice
1/4 cup	extra-virgin olive oil
	freshly ground sea salt and pepper
1 tbsp	grated Parmesan cheese

1 Make the salad: Prepare the beets by chopping off the greens. Steam the beets over medium heat for about 25 minutes, or until a paring knife easily slides into the flesh of the beet. Once the beets are cooked, remove from heat, rinse with cold water, cool, and peel with a paring knife. Cut the beets into eighths.

2 Line a long serving platter with the arugula and layer on the beets, followed by the peas and mint.

3 Make the dressing: Combine the vinegar, lemon juice, and oil in a jar. Shake well and drizzle the desired amount over the salad.

4 Grind salt and pepper generously over the salad. Top with the Parmesan.

SERVES 2 AS A LIGHT MEAL OR 4 AS A SIDE

TARRAGON-YOGURT CHICKEN SALAD

During our final days on a big renovation in the heart of London, England, our client prepared lunch for the design team, and the best part was a fresh and delicious chicken salad. Forgoing the heaviness of mayonnaise, she made hers with yogurt and tarragon . . . and I was hooked! Here's my take on Lizanne's chicken salad. You can use leftovers, but as a quick cheat, I sometimes buy a roasted chicken from the grocer and remove all the meat from the carcass.

1	whole roasted chicken, or 4 grilled or roasted boneless chicken breasts, at room temperature
1/2 cup	Greek yogurt (you can use any yogurt you have on hand, but I find Greek is rich and thick)
2 tbsp	sour cream
1 tbsp	freshly grated lemon zest, plus more as needed
1 tbsp	freshly squeezed lemon juice, plus more as needed
2 tbsp	extra-virgin olive oil
1/4 cup	chopped fresh tarragon, plus more as garnish
	freshly ground sea salt and pepper

1 Chop the cooked chicken into bite-size pieces and put in a mixing bowl.

2 In a smaller bowl, combine the yogurt, sour cream, lemon zest and juice, oil, and chopped tarragon and mix together. Grind in lots of salt and pepper to taste. If desired, add extra lemon zest or juice. The key is to create a dressing that is not too runny.

3 Toss the chicken with the dressing, ensuring the chicken is well coated but not swimming in liquid. If there is leftover dressing, serve it in a bowl on the side in case anyone wants extra.

4 Grind salt and pepper on the chicken and sprinkle with a bit of zest and tarragon for garnish.

SERVES 4

BABY KALE SALAD

Kale is rich in vitamins K, A, and C, as well as antioxidants and fibre. No wonder it's considered a superfood! Combine these leafy greens with some colour, crunch, and zing, and you've got a delicious salad that is satisfying enough to be a main course.

SALAD

½ cup	whole, blanched raw almonds
1 pkg	prewashed organic baby kale
½	apple or pear
1	ripe avocado
½ cup	dried cranberries
¼ cup	crumbled blue cheese (such as Gorgonzola, Roquefort, or Bleu d'Auvergne)

DRESSING

¼ cup	olive oil
¼ cup	red wine vinegar
1 tbsp	whole-grain Dijon mustard
	freshly ground sea salt and pepper

1 Make the salad: Preheat the oven to 300°F. Spread the almonds in a shallow baking pan and roast in the oven for 15 minutes, or until they become golden on the outside. Remove from the oven and cool completely. This can be done ahead of time, and if you like this salad, you may want to roast a larger quantity so you always have some ready. Store the cooled, roasted almonds in an airtight jar.

2 Empty the kale into a large salad bowl.

3 Core the apple half or pear half, then cut into thin slices. Chop the slices into small pieces and sprinkle on the kale.

4 Pit and peel the avocado. Chop into small cubes and add to the salad.

5 Add the cranberries, blue cheese, and almonds.

6 Combine the oil, vinegar, and mustard and mix well. Dress the salad and season to taste with lots of salt and pepper.

SERVES 4 AS A MAIN OR 6 – 8 AS A SIDE

FRESH-FROM-THE-FIELD TOMATO SALAD

Lazy summers call for easy recipes that celebrate the bursting flavours of fresh-from-the-field ingredients. With a medley of vibrant colours and juicy bites, this chopped salad looks great, takes mere minutes to make, and is an easy complement to a variety of summer meals, from burgers to grilled fish.

2	ripe yet firm nectarines
1 cup	grape tomatoes
1 cup	bocconcini (mozzarella pearls)
$\frac{1}{2}$	Vidalia onion
12	large fresh basil leaves
$\frac{1}{4}$ cup	balsamic vinegar
2 tbsp	olive oil
	freshly ground sea salt and pepper

1 Rinse the nectarines, cut in half along the ridge, remove the stone from the fruit, then chop into bite-size cubes. Put the fruit into a medium serving bowl.

2 Rinse the tomatoes and cut in half lengthwise, slice the bocconcini in half, slice the onion, and rinse and roughly chop the basil. Add everything to the bowl.

3 Pour the vinegar into a small pan and bring to a boil over medium-high heat. Reduce the heat once the vinegar starts to bubble and keep cooking until it becomes thick. Watch closely to ensure it doesn't burn.

4 Mix the salad ingredients together in the bowl, drizzle with the olive oil, add lots of salt and pepper, then drizzle the balsamic reduction over the salad before serving.

SERVES 4

EASY WEEKNIGHT FRITTATA

We all have those nights when we're just too wiped to prep anything advanced or gourmet. Instead of dialing up a pizza, you can make a comforting one-pan meal that is packed with veggies, covered in cheese, and loaded with nutrition. It's an easy way to clean out the contents of your crisper drawer or use up leftovers such as roasted veggies or meat. And you can use any combination of flavourful cheeses you have on hand, so this is a great way to use up those little bits too.

6	large eggs
1/2 cup	milk
	freshly ground sea salt and pepper
8	mushrooms, washed and thinly sliced
1 tbsp	extra-virgin olive oil
1/2 cup	fresh corn kernels (or frozen)
6 stems	asparagus, chopped into 1 1/2-inch pieces
1 cup	spinach leaves, washed and dried
1/2 cup	grated sharp cheddar cheese

1 Preheat the oven to 425°F.

2 Combine the eggs and milk in a mixing bowl, beat well, and season with sea salt and pepper.

3 In a medium-size, oven-safe skillet, sauté the mushrooms in the olive oil over medium-high heat for about 5 minutes, until they start to soften, then add the corn and asparagus and continue to sauté for about 3 minutes until the mushrooms have released all their moisture (if the veggies are too wet when you add the eggs, the frittata will be runny).

4 Once the vegetables are done, toss the spinach into the pan and stir quickly to mix it up, then immediately add the egg mixture to the skillet and stir gently once or twice to ensure everything is well blended. Heat for 3 to 4 minutes to start cooking the eggs (but do not stir), then grind salt and pepper on top of the eggs and cover the surface with the cheese.

5 Carefully move the skillet into the oven to finish cooking for about 15 minutes, until the cheese is melted and turning golden brown and the eggs are fully cooked and don't move if you jiggle the pan. You may need to cook for longer depending on the size of your pan and the depth of your frittata.

6 Remove the skillet from the oven, let stand a few minutes, then cut into wedges and serve.

SERVES 2 – 4

GRILLED CITRUS SALMON

I assembled the recipes for this book by asking my friends, my family, and my team at the office to tell me what foods and recipes immediately came to mind when they thought of me in the kitchen. Grilled salmon with mango salsa quickly popped to the top of the list, and for good reason. Summer days call for lighter fare, and I find salmon so easy to cook on the BBQ.

1 tbsp	grated fresh ginger
1	large lime, zest and juice
1 tbsp	orange juice
1 tbsp	low-sodium soy sauce
¼ cup	maple syrup
4	individual salmon fillets (when entertaining, it looks best to serve fillets that are cut about 1 ½ to 2 inches wide)
	freshly ground sea salt and pepper

1 Put the ginger in a measuring cup or small bowl.

2 Grate the zest of the lime (or 2 small ones), then juice it. Add the lime zest and juice to the ginger, along with the orange juice, soy sauce, and maple syrup.

3 Place the fillets in a shallow bowl, add some sea salt and pepper, then pour the marinade over the fish. Allow the fish to marinate for at least 30 minutes. The salmon can be marinated in advance, but it's not necessary. The marinade can be used with any cut of salmon you prefer.

4 When ready to cook, turn all burners on the grill to high. Once it reaches 500°F, turn off the middle burner and place the salmon directly on the middle area of the grill, skin-side down. (You do not want direct heat under the salmon or the skin will catch fire, so if indirect heat is not an option on your BBQ, I would suggest placing the fillets on a piece of aluminum foil.)

5 Cook the fillets for 10 to 12 minutes, depending on whether you prefer them a bit rare or well-done. (Do not turn them over, as they will likely fall apart.) Use a metal spatula to remove the fillets from the grill. I like to slide the metal between the skin and the fish so the skin stays where it is (usually stuck to the grill), and the fish can be presented nicely. Serve with Mango Salsa. I like to also serve them with asparagus or a light green salad to round out the meal.

SERVES 4

MANGO SALSA

I embrace colour and texture in food in the same way I do with homes and rooms. A bright and fresh-looking meal makes me want to dive in and experience the flavours and combinations created by a variety of elements. This mango salsa is summer-fresh delicious, and equally tasty with simple grilled salmon or chicken.

1	mango
4	green onions
1	orange bell pepper
½	red onion
½ pint	grape tomatoes
¼ cup	fresh basil leaves, finely chopped
¼ cup	fresh cilantro, finely chopped
1	lime
¼ cup	olive oil
	freshly ground sea salt and pepper

1 There are two ways to extract the mango fruit. You can slice the halves away from the stone and then score the flesh, flip it inside out, and cut it away from the skin, or you can start by peeling the mango with a potato peeler and then cut the flesh away from the stone to get all the fruit. The key is to get all the fruit and none of the stone. Chop the fruit into bite-size pieces.

2 Trim the ends off the green onion and finely chop the white and light-green parts only.

3 Chop the orange pepper and red onion, and quarter the tomatoes.

4 Combine the mango, orange pepper, tomatoes, green onions, red onion, basil, and cilantro in a mixing bowl and stir gently to combine.

5 Cut the lime in two and squeeze both halves over the ingredients. Pour the oil on top, season with lots of sea salt and pepper, toss to combine, and serve. You can adjust the amount of lime and cilantro to suit your taste buds. Serve with Grilled Citrus Salmon.

SERVES 4 – 6

SAUTÉED CORN WITH CHÈVRE

Our friend Daniel came to visit us at the farm and arrived for the weekend with armloads of groceries. Hurray! Corn was on the menu, and Dan suggested mixing it with chèvre. I admit, at first I was dubious, but the combination of sweet corn with sautéed onions and melted chèvre is a taste sensation. I may never go back to corn on the cob (unless I roll it in chèvre). This is such an easy side dish; try it with any grilled meat or fish. Leftovers, if any, can be tossed into a salad the next day too!

4	ears sweet corn
2 tbsp	olive oil
1/2	large onion (I like the mildness of Vidalia, but red or Spanish onion works too)
1 tbsp	balsamic vinegar
1/4 cup	crumbled chèvre
	freshly ground sea salt and pepper

1 Shuck the corn and cut the kernels off the cob. (I like to lay the corn lengthwise on a cutting board and use a large chef's knife to quickly cut the kernels off, which is less messy than standing the cob on its end.)

2 Heat the oil in a frying pan or cast-iron skillet over medium-high heat. Once it's hot, add the onion and sauté for a few minutes until the onion becomes translucent. Add the vinegar and continue to sauté for a few more minutes, until the onion is browned and caramelized.

3 Add the corn to the pan and mix well. Cook for another 5 to 7 minutes, stirring often so the corn is evenly cooked but not overcooked. As soon as the corn is done (test a kernel to be sure), take it off the heat and set aside.

4 Stir in the chèvre until it is melted and creamy. (When I buy the vacuum-sealed package of chèvre from the grocery store, I tend to use a piece that is about one-third to half of the package.) Add salt and pepper to taste.

SERVES 4 AS A SIDE

CITRUS-HERB GRILLED CHICKEN WITH STONE FRUIT AND YOGURT SAUCE

I often experiment with new ways to prepare some of the staple foods we eat regularly. Grilled chicken is an easy crowd-pleaser for everyday meals at home, but it's also so quick and easy that I find it's an ideal entertaining choice too. Consider serving this if you are having a summer buffet dinner. It doesn't need to be plated piping hot; it's flavoured with basic herbs that may be growing in your garden or window box, and it can be marinated ahead of time so you can be relaxed and ready when guests arrive.

CHICKEN

1/4 cup	fresh flat-leaf parsley
1/2 cup	fresh basil leaves
5	fresh sage leaves
5 sprigs	fresh thyme, leaves stripped from the stems
	juice of 1 lemon
2 tbsp	white balsamic vinegar
	freshly ground sea salt and pepper
1/3 cup	olive oil
6	boneless, skinless chicken breasts

STONE FRUIT

4	stone fruits
1 tbsp	balsamic vinegar
1 tbsp	olive oil

SAUCE

1/3 cup	sour cream
1/3 cup	plain yogurt (Greek yogurt is thickest and best)
1 tbsp	extra-virgin olive oil, plus more as needed
1 tbsp	freshly squeezed lemon juice
3 tbsp	flat-leaf parsley, roughly chopped
3 tbsp	fresh basil, roughly chopped
	freshly ground sea salt and pepper

1 Make the chicken: Chop all the herbs and combine together in a small pitcher or bowl.

2 Add the lemon juice, vinegar, salt, pepper, and oil and mix well.

3 Place the chicken in a shallow baking dish or bowl, pour the marinade over the top, and turn the chicken in the marinade with tongs to ensure each piece is coated well. Let sit for 1 hour or, if making ahead of time, overnight in the refrigerator.

4 While the chicken is marinating, prepare the stone fruit: Slice plums, nectarines, or peaches in half from top to bottom along the rib of the fruit. Remove the pit or stone gently to avoid mashing up the fruit. Freestone peaches, in season, are a great choice for this.

5 Using a paring knife, score an *X* on the inside of the halved fruit to provide a channel for absorbing marinade.

6 Drizzle oil and vinegar into the well left by the pit.

7 When the chicken is ready, bring a gas grill up to 500°F, then turn off the middle burner and cook the chicken over indirect heat for about 4 minutes per side.

8 Grill the fruit alongside the chicken, skin-side down, until the fruit begins to slump. I generally put the fruit on at the same time as the chicken. Transfer to a serving plate.

9 Make the sauce: Mix all the sauce ingredients together and add salt and pepper and a drizzle of oil on top. Serve a large dollop of sauce alongside the grilled chicken and stone fruit.

SERVES 6

APPLE BERRY CRISP

No matter what season it is, I love a crisp for dessert. It's not too sweet and is a refreshing end to a meal. When berries aren't in season, I use a frozen "power fruit blend" of blackberries, cherries, and blueberries. The topping skips the flour that is often used in a traditional crisp, and the result is a crunchy, golden oat crust that is as comforting as an oatmeal cookie.

FRUIT

2	medium to large apples
1/2	lemon, juice and zest
4 cups	mixed fresh or frozen fruit such as blueberries, cherries, blackberries, strawberries, or raspberries

CRISP TOPPING

1/3 cup	butter
1 cup	brown sugar
2 cups	organic whole oats (not quick cooking)
1/2 tsp	ground cinnamon
1/3 cup	maple syrup, plus more if needed

1 Preheat the oven to 350°F.

2 Prepare the fruit: Cut the apples into quarters, core them, then cut in halves or thirds depending on the size of the apples. Put the pieces in a mixing bowl and toss with the lemon juice, then layer them into the bottom of a 6-by-9-inch baking dish. (You can use any size dish you like and add more or less fruit to suit the size of dish you've got. This is a flexible recipe, and you can't go wrong.)

3 Pour the mixed fruit on top of the apples. Sprinkle the lemon zest over all the fruit.

4 Make the crisp topping: In a separate mixing bowl, cut the butter into small slices or cubes so it will soften. Add the brown sugar, oats, and cinnamon to the butter and blend with your hands until the mixture is crumbly. Add the maple syrup.

5 Distribute the crisp topping evenly over the fruit. If your topping looks too dry, you can drizzle a bit more maple syrup over it before you put the crisp in the oven.

6 Cook until the crisp topping is a rich golden tone and the fruit juices are bubbling around the edges of the dish, 45 to 55 minutes. I like to put the crisp in the oven just before dinner begins, so it's hot and ready when the main course is done.

7 Serve with ice cream, or if you want a healthier alternative, mix plain, low-fat Greek yogurt with 1 tablespoon brown sugar per cup of yogurt, then spoon on top of the crisp.

SERVES 8

CHOCOLATE CHIP COOKIES

I've worked a long time to find the ultimate chocolate chip cookie recipe that's not too sweet and is overwhelmingly delicious. I think this is it . . . and the girls agree!

³/₄ cup	butter
¹/₂ cup	brown sugar
¹/₂ cup	cane sugar
2	large eggs
2 tsp	vanilla extract
1 tsp	baking soda
1 tsp	salt
2 cups	Flour Power Blend (pg 205) or cake and pastry flour
1 bag (6 oz)	dark chocolate chips

1 Preheat the oven to 350°F.

2 Combine the butter and the sugars in the bowl of a stand mixer and beat until light and fluffy. Add the eggs and vanilla and beat until completely mixed.

3 Add the baking soda and salt and mix until blended.

4 Slowly add the flour with the mixer on low speed until just combined, then stir in the chocolate chips with a spoon.

5 Drop the batter by spoonfuls onto a baking sheet lined with parchment paper, then flatten each slightly by dipping a spoon in water and pressing down on the cookie with the back side.

6 Bake for 9 to 11 minutes, until the cookies are just golden on top. (This will produce chewy, gooey cookies. Leaving them until they are brown on top will make crunchy cookies. If using the Flour Power Blend, note that the cookies will spread out and run together. Instead of being cakey, they will be light and delicate.)

MAKES ABOUT 30 COOKIES

FALL & WINTER

BERRYLICIOUS WAFFLES (OR PANCAKES)

Asking what the girls want for breakfast on Saturday mornings is a rhetorical question. The answer is always the same: waffles! Preferably swimming in a lake of pure maple syrup (referred to as Lake Maple at our table). Since this was becoming such a regular occurrence, I decided I had to figure out how to make it healthy too. So here's my way of making weekend mornings nutritious as well as delicious. Pass the maple syrup, please!

3	ripe or very ripe bananas
5	large eggs
1 cup	plain yogurt
1/2 – 3/4 cup	milk
2 tsp	vanilla extract
1 tbsp	baking powder
1/4 tsp	baking soda
1/2 tsp	salt
2 1/2 cups	Flour Power Blend (see pg 205)
1/2 cup	unsweetened coconut (optional)
1 cup	fresh or frozen raspberries or strawberries (or a mix of both)
	oil, for the waffle maker

1 Purée the bananas, eggs, and yogurt in a blender (my preferred method for fastest prep and cleanup) on medium-high for about 1 minute, until smooth and frothy. Add the milk, vanilla, baking powder, baking soda, and salt and purée again for 30 to 45 seconds.

2 Pour the contents of the blender into a large bowl and add the flour blend, stirring just until combined. Add the coconut (if using) and stir once or twice. The batter shouldn't be too runny or too thick, so add extra milk if needed. (This recipe also works for pancakes, which require a batter that is a bit thinner.)

3 Tear the raspberries into smaller pieces if using fresh, or crumble them into the batter if frozen. Mix until just blended.

4 Brush some oil (I use olive oil for everything, but you may prefer the taste of a light vegetable oil) onto the waffle maker plates. Pour 1 to 1 1/2 cups of batter into the waffle maker and cook according to the directions of your machine. If you use the Flour Power Blend, your waffles will have a rich golden hue. I find the use of ground flax makes them light and airy.

MAKES ABOUT TWELVE 4-BY-4-INCH WAFFLES

COSMIC SANDWICH

Some mornings just call for a breakfast sandwich — an entire breakfast between two sides of a freshly toasted bagel. But my Cosmic Sandwich isn't just any drive-through adventure. It's loaded up with protein and veggies to make it an irresistible morning treat for a hearty start to the day. The taste is out of this world!

PER SANDWICH

2 slices	good-quality bacon from the butcher
1	bagel
2 tbsp	grated sharp cheddar cheese
1 tsp	mayonnaise
1 tsp	whole-grain Dijon mustard
1 – 2	eggs (depending on how hungry your gang is)
¼	avocado, sliced into thin wedges
2	grape tomatoes, sliced into thin pieces
6	arugula leaves (or lettuce of your choice)
	freshly ground sea salt and pepper

1 Cook the bacon until crispy, then set aside. Drain most of the fat from the pan, but reserve just enough to fry the eggs.

2 Slice a bagel in half, toast lightly, then cover one half with cheese. Spread the mayonnaise and mustard on the other half and set aside.

3 Heat the broiler. Place the bagel half with cheese on it under the broiler until the cheese is melted.

4 Meanwhile, cook the eggs over easy. You can leave the yolks a bit runny if desired, or cook until firm.

5 Assemble the sandwich using the bagel half with the melted cheese as the base, then stack on the egg(s), bacon, avocado, tomatoes, and arugula. Season with salt and pepper to taste and top with the remaining bagel half.

MAKES 1 SANDWICH

LEEK-ZUCCHINI CHEESE TART

Over a decade ago, my mom and I started making this tart during the Christmas holidays, and it's become a staple for our winter feasts. You might think working with phyllo is intimidating, but it's actually fun and easy to use. The trick is to work with a partner so you can move quickly before the phyllo dries up and tears. With glasses of wine in hand while preparing, my mom and I have had many a giggle while whipping up this savoury tart.

4	leeks
2	small to medium zucchini
1/2	red onion
1 tbsp	olive oil
4	eggs
3/4 cup	low-fat ricotta cheese
3/4 cup	crumbled light Greek feta cheese
3/4 cup	grated Parmesan cheese
1/4 cup	fresh basil, chopped
1/4 cup	fresh parsley, chopped
	freshly ground sea salt and pepper
2 tbsp	butter, melted
2 tbsp	olive oil
1 pkg	frozen phyllo

1 Chop off the leek root and remove the first layer of outside leaves. Slice the leeks in half and run under cold water to remove any dirt stuck in the leaves. Dry and chop into pieces.

2 Trim the ends off the zucchini, slice into quarters, then chop into small pieces. Slice the half onion in half, trim the base off, then roughly chop into pieces.

3 Warm the oil over medium heat in a large frying pan, then add the leeks and sauté for a few minutes, until they soften slightly. Add the zucchini and onion and continue to sauté for about 10 minutes more, until the leeks are soft and the zucchini and onion have gone a bit clear. Remove the pan from the heat and pour its contents into a large bowl. Set aside.

4 Meanwhile, combine the eggs, ricotta, feta, and Parmesan in a large bowl and mix well.

5 Pour the egg mixture over the leek mixture, add the herbs, stir to combine all the ingredients, and season well with salt and pepper.

6 Preheat the oven to 350°F. Combine the butter in a small bowl with the olive oil.

7 Now you are ready to assemble the tart. I've always made this in a basic 9-by-13-inch baking sheet, as I like the way it makes maximum use of the phyllo sheets, is easy to assemble, and feeds a crowd. Start by laying the first sheet of phyllo lengthwise down the pan, and brush a bit of the butter and oil onto the phyllo with a pastry brush. Then lay down four or five more sheets in the same way, keeping the edges fairly even and brushing with the butter and oil in between. The extra phyllo should just hang over the edges of the pan.

8 Pour the leek mixture onto the phyllo and gently spread it out evenly with a spatula.

9 To form the top crust, layer five or six phyllo sheets over the leek mixture, applying a bit of the butter and oil between each sheet.

10 To finish it off, fold up the extra phyllo that hangs over the edges of the pan and brush it with a bit of the oil and butter. Put the tart in the oven to bake for 40 minutes, or until the crust looks crispy and golden brown.

11 Cut into pieces using a chef's knife or pizza cutter and serve alongside meat or salad. It keeps well in the refrigerator for a couple of days and can be reheated in the oven.

SERVES 8 – 12 AS A SIDE

UNFORGETTABLE SPICED NUTS

A long time ago I shared one of my entertaining secrets with *House & Home* magazine for a holiday feature. Almost a decade later, my spiced nuts remain a popular online recipe during the holidays. They are easy to prepare, impossible to resist, and make a great homemade gourmet gift when packaged in an airtight jar with a pretty tag. In other words, no holiday is complete without them.

---

1 tbsp	extra-virgin olive oil
2 tbsp	balsamic vinegar
1/4 cup	demerara sugar
1 tsp	ground cumin
1 tsp	paprika
1 tsp	cayenne pepper
1 tsp	sea salt
1 cup	raw whole almonds
1 cup	pecan halves

1 Preheat the oven to 350°F.

2 Stir the olive oil, balsamic vinegar, and demerara sugar together in a frying pan or saucepan over medium-low heat.

3 Sprinkle in the cumin, paprika, cayenne, and salt and mix well.

4 Add the almonds and pecans, stir to coat, then cook until the mixture becomes sticky, about 5 minutes.

5 Spread the nuts on a baking sheet lined with parchment paper and bake for 15 to 20 minutes, or until crunchy.

6 Let cool and serve at room temperature. The spiced nuts will keep for a few weeks in an airtight container.

MAKES 2 CUPS

HERB-MARINATED CHÈVRE

When impromptu guests show up at your door, it's good to be able to whip up a quick snack. My mom has been making this marinated chèvre for about twenty years, and I never tire of it. The longer it sits, the better it gets, though you may not get a chance to find out!

1 piece	chèvre, about 1 ½ inches thick
1 tsp	herbes de Provence
1 tbsp	extra-virgin olive oil
4 – 5	fresh basil leaves
	freshly ground sea salt and pepper
	ciabatta, baguette, or crackers, for serving

1 Place the chèvre in a small, decorative serving bowl.

2 Sprinkle the herbes de Provence over the cheese, then pour the olive oil on top.

3 Finely chop the basil and mound it on top of the cheese. Grind pepper and sea salt to taste over the top.

4 Serve with a fresh crusty bread or the crackers of your choice.

SERVES 4

SPINACH AND BLUE CHEESE SALAD

Dark, leafy greens such as spinach are packed with vitamins and antioxidants, are heart healthy, and best of all make the ideal base for a salad bowl full of yumminess. You can serve this salad as a side with steak or chicken, but I often make it as the main event for a light dinner and think it makes an ideal lunch choice.

SALAD

1	package organic baby spinach
1	small avocado
¼ cup	shelled fresh peas (optional)
¼ cup	shelled walnut halves (or pieces)
¼	crisp pear
¼ cup	red or green grapes
¼ cup	high-quality blue cheese (such as Gorgonzola, Roquefort, or Bleu d'Auvergne)
	freshly ground sea salt and pepper

DRESSING

½	lemon
¼ cup	balsamic vinegar
⅓ cup	extra-virgin olive oil
1 tbsp	honey

1 Make the salad: Put the spinach in a large salad bowl.

2 Pit and peel the avocado and chop into bite-size pieces. Sprinkle over the spinach along with the peas (if using) and walnuts.

3 Cut the pear into small slivers and slice the grapes in half. Throw them into the bowl.

4 Break the blue cheese into small crumbles or cubes (depending on how moist it is) and distribute evenly over the greens.

5 Make the dressing: Juice the lemon half into a small glass jar with a lid. Add the vinegar, oil, and honey and shake vigorously until emulsified.

6 Season the salad with freshly ground sea salt and pepper. Add the dressing, toss, and serve.

SERVES 4 AS A LUNCH SALAD

BLACK FOREST HAM AND GRUYÈRE TOASTS

With a busy household, I often find that I'm trying to figure out how to create tasty meal ideas when supplies are running low. Thankfully, melted cheese can make even the simplest fare seem so much more gourmet. To provide a hearty bite to accompany a salad or soup at lunch, I'll broil a pan of these little treats. Served hot, they can take the chill off any day.

12 slices	baguette (sliced on an angle)
2 tbsp	mayonnaise
2 tbsp	whole-grain Dijon mustard
12 thin slices	Black Forest ham
1 cup	grated Gruyère cheese
	freshly ground pepper

1 Lay the bread slices close together on a baking sheet.

2 Mix the mayonnaise and mustard together in a small bowl, then spread a bit on each slice of bread.

3 Lay a slice of ham on top of each slice of bread, then sprinkle the cheese over the ham to cover it completely. Grind some fresh pepper over the top to taste.

4 Heat the broiler. Place the baking sheet under the broiler for a minute or two, until the cheese is bubbling and melted. Serve with a delicious salad.

SERVES 4 – 6

FESTIVE ARUGULA SALAD

This salad is a holiday staple in my family. A friend's husband always hopes this will be on the dinner menu at our place . . . and it often is! Colourful and refreshing pomegranate, peppery and fresh arugula, and crunchy and sweet candied pecans make this a salad worth repeating.

SALAD

1 tbsp	butter
1 tbsp	brown sugar
1 tbsp	balsamic vinegar
1 cup	pecan pieces
6 cups	baby arugula
³/₄ cup	goat cheese
3	green onions, thinly sliced
	seeds of ¹/₂ pomegranate

DRESSING

¹/₂ cup	extra-virgin olive oil
3 tbsp	balsamic vinegar
1 tbsp	fresh squeezed lemon juice
	freshly ground sea salt and pepper

1 Make the salad: Melt the butter in a skillet over medium heat, then add the brown sugar and balsamic vinegar. Stir quickly to combine, being careful not to burn.

2 Add the pecans, stir to coat well, and sauté for a couple of minutes, stirring constantly, until the coating on the nuts begins to caramelize. Remove from the heat and allow to cool.

3 Place the arugula in a large salad bowl. Crumble the goat cheese evenly over the greens, then top with the green onions, pomegranate seeds, and cooled pecans.

4 Make the dressing: Combine the ingredients for the dressing in a jar with a lid. Shake well, then drizzle over the salad, toss, and serve.

5 Season to taste with sea salt and pepper.

NOTE: If you are serving this as the starter course for a dinner party, plate the salad on individual dishes, then drizzle with the salad dressing just before serving so it looks fresh and beautiful.

SERVES 6 – 8 AS AN APPETIZER

COMFY, COZY CARBONARA

On a chilly weeknight in the middle of winter, if I ask Alexander what he feels like having for dinner, he will probably say, "Something cozy and yummy," and I know exactly what this means: pasta carbonara! What could be more comforting when the mercury dips than piping-hot pasta covered in a smooth and delicious sauce of bacon, eggs, cream, and cheese? Too decadent for you? I've tailored the classic carbonara recipe to include vitamin-rich veggies to eliminate any guilt!

4 – 6 slices	side bacon
12	medium to large brown mushrooms
8 spears	asparagus
1/2	Vidalia onion
	freshly ground pepper
4 cups	dry pasta
2	eggs
2	egg yolks
1/2 cup	heavy cream
3/4 cup	freshly grated Parmesan cheese
2 tbsp	chopped fresh parsley

1 Fill a pasta pot with salted water and bring to a boil on the stovetop.

2 Meanwhile, chop the raw bacon into pieces about $3/4$ inch wide and cook in a large frying pan until browned and crispy.

3 While the bacon is cooking, thinly slice the mushrooms and chop the asparagus into 1-inch-long pieces.

4 Remove the bacon from the pan and set aside. Drain most of the bacon fat from the pan, reserving about 1 tablespoon for cooking.

5 Chop the onion and add it to the frying pan. Sauté about 3 minutes before adding the mushrooms. Add pepper to taste. Cook until the mushrooms have stopped releasing moisture.

6 Cook the pasta in the boiling water, following the instructions on the box. You can use any type of pasta, but I enjoy how penne holds the saucy goodness inside the tubes. When the pasta is almost done, add the asparagus pieces to the water and cook together for 2 minutes or less (so the asparagus is just cooked and not mushy).

7 Put the eggs, egg yolks, and cream in a large bowl and beat. Add $1/2$ cup of the grated Parmesan (save the rest for topping) and mix well.

8 Return the bacon to the frying pan with the mushrooms and onions and stir together, making sure they are hot.

9 Drain (do not rinse) the pasta and asparagus. Dump the bacon, mushrooms, and onions from the frying pan, as well as the pasta and asparagus, into the hot pasta pot. Pour in the cream mixture, stir, and leave covered for a couple of minutes. Do not put the pan back on the burner, as the heat will turn the cream sauce to scrambled eggs. The heat from the pot and pasta is enough to just cook the eggs and give the sauce a smooth and creamy consistency.

10 Serve in bowls, sprinkle with parsley, and top with a bit more Parmesan. Season with some sea salt and pepper.

SERVES 4 – 6

BEN'S BASIC TOMATO SAUCE

Looking for a quick and easy recipe for homemade pasta sauce? This is it! On a rainy day at the cottage, my brother Ben showed me his awesome and easy recipe for tomato sauce that can be used on pasta, pizzas, and more.

2 tbsp	olive oil
3 cloves	garlic
2 tins	whole, peeled tomatoes (preferably San Marzano)
	freshly ground sea salt and pepper
10	chopped fresh basil leaves, or a 1 – 2 tbsp chunk of the Basil Purée (pg 263)

1 Warm the oil in a large, deep frying pan or stockpot over medium-high heat.

2 Peel and dice the garlic cloves and cook quickly in the oil, then add the tomatoes just as the garlic begins to turn golden (do not let it burn).

3 Season with lots of salt and pepper and bring the tomatoes to a boil over medium-high heat, then reduce the heat to medium-low and let it simmer for 20 to 25 minutes. If you've got a lid big enough to cover the pan, you may want to cover it for half the time so your kitchen isn't spattered with sauce, but it needs to remain uncovered for at least half the time to reduce the liquid. I like to use the back of a wooden spoon to help mash down and mush up the tomatoes once they start cooking. The sauce is done when the tomatoes have formed a nice chunky sauce. When almost finished, add chopped basil or Basil Purée. Serve with pasta or on a pizza. Save any extra in an airtight container for up to a week, or pop in the freezer so it's ready when you need a meal in a hurry!

SERVES 6

KID-FRIENDLY CHICKEN MEATBALLS

I've got a house with little people who would happily gobble up plain pasta with cheese every night of the week if given the chance, so I'm constantly trying to sneak a bit more nutrition into everything I serve. These chicken meatballs take mere minutes to make and can cook in the pan while the pasta is cooking in the pot. As an adult alternative, serve them alongside a gourmet green salad with a simple vinaigrette, and you'll have something to please all your fussy eaters, big and small.

1 ½ lbs	lean ground chicken
¾ cup	panko bread crumbs
½ tsp	freshly ground sea salt
½ tsp	freshly ground pepper
1 tbsp	chopped fresh flat-leaf parsley
1 tbsp	chopped fresh sage
2 cloves	garlic, minced (optional)
1 cup	grated Parmesan cheese
1	large egg
1 tbsp	whole-grain Dijon mustard
1 tbsp	low-sodium soy or teriyaki sauce
1 tbsp	extra-virgin olive oil

1 Place the ground chicken in a bowl and add the salt and pepper.

2 In a separate bowl, mix the herbs, garlic, Parmesan cheese, egg, mustard, soy sauce, and bread crumbs together. Stir well, then pour over the chicken and mix until fully blended. If you've got fussy eaters, feel free to skip the garlic.

3 Roll the mixture into small balls (about the size of Ping-Pong balls).

4 Heat the olive oil in a large skillet over medium heat. When the oil is hot, add the meatballs and cook for a few minutes until golden brown. Turn the meatballs to cook evenly on all sides and remove them from the pan when firm.

5 Serve with pasta and Ben's Basic Tomato Sauce, or with a hearty salad.

MAKES ABOUT 30 SMALL MEATBALLS

GRILLED FLANK STEAK WITH GORGONZOLA MUSHROOMS

For years I never considered the lowly flank steak as a gourmet grilling choice, but I'm now converted. It's an easy cut to marinate and prep quickly and works well when you are entertaining a crowd, since you can slice it into long, thin strips. The key is to cook it quick and hot and serve it with a tasty accompaniment for easy (and inexpensive) entertaining.

STEAK

2 lbs	flank steak (look for one with even thickness to ensure best grilling and consistent rareness throughout)
1 tbsp	olive oil
	salt and pepper

MUSHROOMS

2 cups	brown button mushrooms
1 tbsp	olive oil
	salt and pepper
1 tbsp	balsamic vinegar
1/2 cup	blue cheese (such as Gorgonzola, Roquefort, or Bleu d'Auvergne)
	Dijon mustard or fresh horseradish, for serving

1 Prepare the steak: Remove the steak from the refrigerator at least 1 hour before you are planning to grill. Drizzle the oil over the steak, massaging it into both sides of the meat.

2 Grind salt and pepper over the beef, and leave it to sit for 1 hour.

3 Make the mushrooms: Rinse and drain the mushrooms, and slice thinly.

4 Warm the olive oil in a frying pan over medium-high heat and add the mushrooms, turning frequently. Liberally grind on salt and pepper while the mushrooms cook, then turn the heat down to medium and add the vinegar.

5 Cook the mushrooms until they've sweated out most of the liquid and turned a nice, rich brown. Remove from the heat and crumble the blue cheese evenly over the mushrooms.

6 When ready to grill the beef, turn your gas grill to high on all burners. Once it reaches 450°F, turn the middle burner off while leaving the other two burners on high. Cook the beef in the centre of the grill so it is over indirect heat for 3 to 4 minutes per side. Do not overcook it, as it will become tough! Pull it off the grill and leave it to rest for a few minutes, then slice it thinly and plate.

7 Heat the broiler. Place the pan of mushrooms under your oven broiler until the cheese melts and bubbles.

8 Spoon the mushrooms beside the beef slices. Serve with Dijon mustard or fresh horseradish.

SERVES 4

MUSTARD AND ZA'ATAR ROASTED CHICKEN

Harvest menus go hand in hand with roasted chicken, and few main courses are easier to prepare. If roasting chicken in the oven is simple, moving it to the barbecue is a snap. I no longer use the oven when roasted chicken is on the menu. If you love crispy skin, tender meat, and zero cleanup, this recipe will make you a barbecue enthusiast in no time. The dressing is quick to prep and is flavoured with za'atar (a Lebanese spice that adds a richness to poultry and roasted vegetables).

1 tbsp	whole-grain Dijon mustard
1 tbsp	Dijon mustard
1 tbsp	olive oil
1 tsp	za'atar
1	lime, zested

CHICKEN

1	roasting chicken
1	lemon
	freshly ground sea salt and pepper

1 Prepare the dressing by mixing the mustards, oil, za'atar, and lime zest in a small bowl to create a paste. Spread the paste evenly on the skin of the raw chicken. This can be set aside to marinate for up to an hour, but it's still flavourful if cooked immediately.

2 Slice a lemon in half and put one half (or both) in the chicken's cavity.

3 Grind salt and pepper on top of the chicken.

4 Turn the barbecue on high. Once it reaches 500°F, turn off the middle burner.

5 Place the chicken on a sheet of aluminum foil. Turn up the edges of the foil to create a "pan" so the juices and fat don't drip into the grill and cause a flame-up.

6 Lift the foil and chicken together and place them on the centre of the grill where the heat is turned off. Barbecue the chicken until the skin looks crispy and golden, and the juices from the chicken run clear (generally 45 to 60 minutes for a 4- to 5-pound chicken).

7 Turn off the barbecue and let the flames go out before removing the chicken from the grill. Transfer the chicken to a cutting board using a pair of large forks. Carve and serve.

SERVES 4

ROASTED HEIRLOOM CARROTS

You just can't go wrong with root vegetables as a side for any meal. I like them roasted because it is minimal effort with maximum taste. Heirloom carrots come in a range of colours and are packed with flavour.

12	whole heirloom carrots
	freshly ground sea salt and pepper
1 tbsp	balsamic vinegar
2 tbsp	olive oil
	squeeze of lemon juice
	fresh parsley or basil, roughly chopped, for garnish

1 Preheat the oven to 350°F.

2 Arrange the carrots in a baking dish or pan. Season with salt and pepper, then toss with the vinegar and oil.

3 Roast on the middle rack of the oven for about 35 minutes, until the skin looks roasted and the flesh of the carrots is well cooked.

4 For a fresh taste, cut a lemon in half and give it a good squeeze over the carrots, then transfer the contents of the pan to a serving plate and garnish with parsley or basil (or both!). These make a great addition to a roast chicken or beef dish.

SERVES 4

BRUSSELS SPROUTS WITH BACON, LIME, AND MAPLE SYRUP

I loathed brussels sprouts for decades (sorry, Dad), but now I cook them as often as I can. They're a good source of protein, iron, and potassium. Best of all, they are a cinch to prepare. If there are any leftovers, use them to dip in fondue, or chop them up and add to a salad.

4 cups	brussels sprouts
1 tbsp	balsamic vinegar
2 tbsp	olive oil
2 tbsp	orange juice
1 tbsp	grain mustard
	freshly ground salt and pepper
4 – 5	bacon strips

DRESSING

1	lime
1 tbsp	maple syrup
1 tbsp	olive oil

1 Preheat the oven to 400°F. Rinse the brussels sprouts, trim the bases off, then slice in half lengthwise and put in a medium bowl.

2 Mix the vinegar, oil, orange juice, and mustard. Pour over the brussels sprouts and toss well to coat them evenly.

3 Grind salt and pepper over the sprouts and mix again, then transfer to a baking dish for roasting. You can use a nonstick, glass, or ceramic dish. I like to use a ceramic dish, as it holds the heat and can be transferred directly to the table or buffet for casual, family-style dining.

4 Lay the strips of bacon lengthwise over the sprouts (use more or fewer strips as desired). This will allow the bacon to get crispy while keeping the sprouts from getting dried out. Roast for 40 minutes.

5 Make the dressing: While the sprouts are roasting, grate the zest of an entire lime into a small bowl, then squeeze out the juice into the bowl. Stir in the maple syrup and olive oil.

6 Once the bacon is getting crispy, remove the pan from the oven, and transfer the bacon to a cutting board. Chop the bacon into pieces and toss it with the sprouts and the dressing. Season with additional salt and pepper.

SERVES 4 AS A SIDE

SMASHED FETA POTATOES

My brother, Ben, introduced my taste buds to the irresistible combination of melted feta on potatoes. This recipe is my foolproof entertaining solution. Even if you think you've made too many, there rarely seem to be leftovers. No matter how often I make this, people are always asking for it. You can use any type of potato you like, but I find that fingerling potatoes are the best.

1 ½ - 2 lbs	fingerling potatoes
2 tbsp	Basil Purée (see recipe below)
¼ cup	red onion, diced
4 tbsp	olive oil
	freshly ground sea salt and pepper
½ - ¾ cup	crumbled feta cheese

1 Preheat the oven to 425°F.

2 Steam the potatoes over medium-high heat on the stovetop for 12 to 15 minutes until cooked (or when a sharp paring knife slides into the flesh of the potato). Remove from the heat and toss into a large bowl.

3 While the potatoes are cooking, combine the Basil Purée, red onion, and 2 tablespoons of the olive oil in a bowl, pour over the potatoes once cooked, and toss well with lots of salt and pepper.

4 Line a baking sheet with parchment paper and spread out the potatoes on the sheet. Cover them with another piece of parchment paper and press down with your hand to flatten them (if they are still too warm to do this with your hand, you can use a mug or bowl with a flat bottom to press down). The goal is to slightly flatten the potatoes and break the skin on top so the cheese will melt into them. Remove the top piece of parchment paper.

6 Sprinkle the feta cheese over the potatoes. (I usually use a 200-gram package of Greek feta that is widely available in grocery stores. I find the Greek feta is more moist than regular feta, so it melts better.) Drizzle the potatoes with the remaining 2 tablespoons of oil, then sprinkle the feta on top.

7 Place the potatoes on your oven's upper rack and roast for about 20 to 25 minutes, or until the potatoes are golden and the feta is melted.

SERVES 6

EVER-FRESH BASIL PURÉE

Fresh herbs are plentiful in the summer, and easy to grow in your garden, but they can get pricey in the winter. My mom keeps a variety of puréed herbs in her freezer year-round so every recipe can have the rich flavour of fresh herbs even when they aren't growing in the garden.

1 bunch	fresh basil, washed and dried
¼ cup	extra-virgin olive oil

1 Toss the fresh basil into the bowl of a food processor, stems and leaves included (you can pull the leaves off and discard the stems if you prefer, but I just whip it all together).

2 Add the oil and process until all the leaves are chopped up finely.

3 Scoop the purée out into a zip-top freezer bag. Squeeze the bag to remove all the air, then flatten the bag to create an even layer.

4 Keep the bag in the freezer and break off a piece of frozen purée any time you have a recipe that calls for fresh herbs. Alternatively, you can put the purée into small ice-cube trays, but I find using the bag is faster and easier. Try this with other herbs such as parsley, cilantro, or dill.

MAKES ½ CUP

ZESTY WILD RICE SALAD

I know most households put stuffing and gravy high on the holiday-buffet wish list, but trying new culinary adventures is always welcome in our household. My brother, Ben, made this wild rice salad one year to accompany the turkey along with a medley of other flavourful adventures in vegetables, and I thought it was a refreshing change to the ordinary. This dish is served cool or at room temperature, so it's great if you find timing the presentation of a meal to be a challenge. I'm not suggesting you should skip the potatoes and gravy, but why not take a walk on the wild (rice) side for your next entertaining feast?

SALAD

1 cup	wild rice
1 cup	red rice
1	pomegranate
4	green onions
¼ cup	roughly chopped fresh cilantro
¼ cup	roughly chopped fresh parsley
¼ cup	pine nuts
⅓ cup	roasted shelled pumpkin seeds

DRESSING

1 tbsp	lemon or lime zest
¼ cup	freshly squeezed lime juice
2 tbsp	freshly squeezed lemon juice
¼ cup	olive oil
1 tbsp	grain mustard
1 tbsp	maple syrup
	freshly ground sea salt and pepper

1 Make the salad: Cook the rice in separate saucepans according to the package directions. (Since they call for different cooking times, they can't be combined.)

2 Once cooked, drain the rice well so it is not sitting in liquid.

3 Cut the pomegranate in half and turn it inside out to remove the seeds from the skin. (If you don't have pomegranate, you can substitute dried cranberries. I've also used tart plums or raisins. You just need some fruit to make it juicy and refreshing, so feel free to experiment.)

4 Roughly chop the white and light-green parts of the green onions. Combine in a bowl along with the cilantro, parsley, and pomegranate seeds and set aside.

5 Preheat the oven to 300°F. Roast the pine nuts in a baking dish or pan for about 10 to 12 minutes until they're golden on the outside.

6 Combine the wild and red rice together in a large bowl.

7 Toss with the cilantro mix, pine nuts, and pumpkin seeds.

8 Make the dressing: In a bowl, combine all the ingredients for the dressing. I often make dressing in a lidded jar so I can dump all the ingredients in and shake vigorously to blend them (this makes it easy to store extra dressing in the fridge too). Zest the lemon or lime first, then juice it so there is no waste. Pour the dressing over the salad and toss well to ensure the rice is evenly coated. Season to taste with salt and pepper.

SERVES 8 – 10 AS A SIDE

BAKED EGGPLANT À LA SUSU

Do you avoid cooking eggplant because it seems complicated (or doesn't taste great)? This recipe, designed by my mom, makes baked eggplant a cozy comfort food wrapped up in tomato sauce and topped with molten cheese. The best part is that it barely takes any time to prep and can then be tucked in the oven to simmer away while you pull together the rest of the meal.

1	medium-large eggplant
1 tbsp	red wine
1 tbsp	balsamic vinegar
1 tbsp	olive oil
	freshly ground sea salt and pepper
1	jar tomato purée (not tomato sauce)
1 tsp	za'atar
1/2 cup	grated mozzarella cheese (or whatever leftover cheese you have on hand)
1 tbsp	roughly chopped fresh basil
1 tbsp	roughly chopped flat-leaf parsley

1 Preheat the oven to 350°F.

2 Slice the ends off the eggplant and cut it into eighths lengthwise to create long wedges.

3 Arrange the pieces in a microwave-safe dish and microwave on high for 8 to 10 minutes, until the eggplant is soft.

4 Transfer the strips of eggplant to a 6-by-9-inch baking dish (glass, ceramic, or enamel).

5 Drizzle the wine, vinegar, and olive oil over the eggplant so they soak in, and grind salt and pepper on top. The wine is not critical, but if you have some old wine left over, it adds a nice flavour. Use red wine vinegar if you don't have wine.

6 Mix the tomato purée with the za'atar (if you don't have za'atar, you can use herbes de Provence or just plain thyme).

7 Pour the tomato purée over the eggplant until it is completely covered. Cover the dish with aluminum foil and bake for about 30 minutes, or until the tomato sauce is bubbling around the edges.

8 Once the sauce is hot and bubbling, remove the foil and sprinkle the grated cheese on top. Turn the oven temperature up to 400°F and return the dish to the oven for about 12 minutes (or until the cheese is melted and starting to brown slightly). Garnish with the parsley and basil.

SERVES 4 – 6

ROASTED SWEET POTATO SALAD

My approach to food and entertaining is a lot like my direction with design: I like fresh, simple, and creative ideas. While I love the classics, I like a little reinvention and imagination, especially during the holidays. My brother, Ben, lives in London, England, and has brought some great recipes home for the holidays. This salad has been part of our Christmas feast ever since he first made it. Instead of the old standby starches to accompany a winter meal, this salad is a veritable explosion of unexpected flavours.

SALAD

3	medium to large sweet potatoes
1/4 cup	olive oil
	salt and pepper
2 cups	baby kale, washed and dried
1/2 cup	pecans
1	pomegranate
4	green onions
1/2 cup	cilantro
1/2 cup	roasted shelled pumpkin seeds

DRESSING

2 tbsp	grated fresh ginger
1/2 cup	freshly squeezed lemon juice
1/2 cup	olive oil
1/3 cup	maple syrup
	freshly ground sea salt and pepper

1 Make the salad: Preheat the oven to 350°F. Wash the sweet potatoes, trim off the ends, then chop into bite-size cubes or pieces. Toss them in the oil, season with salt and pepper, and spread them out evenly on a nonstick baking sheet. Roast for 35 to 40 minutes or until they look browned, but remove them before the edges start to burn. Reduce the oven temperature to 300°F. Allow the sweet potatoes to cool. (They do not need to be served hot, which is another reason I think this dish is a winner for entertaining.)

2 While the potatoes are roasting, prepare the rest of the ingredients. Line the bottom of a wide, shallow serving bowl with the baby kale. (You can do this without the kale, but I enjoy the crunch and freshness of some greens with any meal, and this makes a nice presentation bed too.)

3 Place the pecans in a baking dish and roast in the oven for about 10 minutes, then remove the dish and allow the pecans to cool.

4 Remove the pomegranate seeds from the shell and keep in a bowl until needed. Chop the white and light-green parts of the green onions and add to the pomegranate seeds. Roughly chop the cilantro and add to the bowl. (This gives the salad a fresh and vibrant flavour.)

5 Make the dressing: Combine the ginger, lemon juice, oil, and maple syrup in a measuring cup or jar and mix well.

6 To assemble the salad, spread the sweet potatoes over the kale, followed by the pomegranate seeds, cilantro, green onions, pecans, and pumpkin seeds. Evenly distribute the dressing over the entire dish.

7 Season the salad with salt and pepper, toss, and serve.

SERVES 6 – 8 AS A SIDE

MASHED POTATO AND SWEET POTATO BAKE

In an attempt to up the ante on the average mashed potato, I experimented with combining the old standby white potato with the amped-up flavour of sweet potatoes. If you're looking for a make-ahead, oven-to-table dish for family-style meals, this is a great option. Instead of butter, I like to use cream cheese when mashing them. Sometimes the best part of any dish is the sauce that accompanies it. That's definitely the case here. A mix of sour cream and Greek yogurt with lemon and cilantro takes the end result to a new level.

MASH

2	medium to large sweet potatoes
4	medium to large white potatoes (so you have equal parts sweet and regular potato)
2 tbsp	light cream cheese
2 tbsp	olive oil, plus more as needed
1/4 cup	milk
1/2 tsp	chili paste (or chili flakes)
1 tbsp	Basil Purée (pg 263)
	freshly ground sea salt and pepper
1/2 cup	grated Parmesan cheese

SAUCE

3	green onions
1/3 cup	fresh cilantro
3 tbsp	sour cream
3 tbsp	Greek yogurt
1 tbsp	freshly squeezed lemon juice
1 tbsp	olive oil
	freshly ground sea salt and pepper

1 Make the mash: Preheat the oven to 400°F.

2 Wash the sweet potatoes and potatoes, trim off the ends, and chop into big chunks. Steam over medium-high heat for 12 to 15 minutes, until fully cooked. (Check by sticking a paring knife into the side of the flesh.) You do not need to peel the skin off.

3 Drain the water from the saucepan, toss the sweet potatoes and potatoes in, and mash slightly. Add the cream cheese, olive oil, milk, chili paste, and Basil Purée and season well with salt and pepper. Continue to mash until everything is well blended and smooth. (It won't be completely smooth, but the goal is to get it well blended.)

4 Spread the mash into a baking dish, drizzle lightly with a bit of olive oil, and sprinkle the Parmesan cheese all over the top.

5 Bake for 15 to 20 minutes just before serving.

6 Make the sauce: Chop the green onions, using the white and light-green parts only, and roughly chop the cilantro. In a bowl, combine the green onions, cilantro, sour cream, yogurt, lemon juice, and oil, mix together, and season with salt and pepper.

7 Serve a scoop of the mash with a good dollop of sauce.

SERVES 6 – 8 AS A SIDE

VERY VEGGIE LASAGNA

If you looked up the definition of comfort food, I'm sure you'd find lasagna listed. When I've got time on a Sunday afternoon, I like to make up a big pan that serves as a cozy Sunday supper and leftovers to coast into the beginning of the week. (Lasagna is absolutely one of those dishes that makes for awesome leftovers.) In my view, the best part isn't the noodles, it's the layers, so I use my lasagna as a way to get as many veggies as possible into a single pan of delicious and nutritious comfort. To assemble the final product, make it in one big baking dish or pan (such as an 8-by-14-inch), or have some fun and create individual servings in oven-safe dishes. The only rule here is to enjoy it. Use more veggies, if you wish, and make extra sauce, but this is a good guideline to get you started.

8	medium carrots
3 – 4	medium-size zucchini
1	large Vidalia onion
4 cups	brown mushrooms
2 tbsp	olive oil
2 cloves	garlic
1 tbsp	balsamic vinegar
1 tsp	za'atar
	freshly ground sea salt and pepper
2 large tins	ground tomatoes
1 tbsp	Basil Purée (pg 263)
1 cup	spinach
1 tub (300g or 10 oz)	ricotta cheese
1 ball (8 oz)	mozzarella cheese
1 pkg	oven-ready lasagna noodles
1/2 cup	freshly grated Parmesan cheese

1 Preheat the oven to 350°F.

2 Cut the ends off the carrots and zucchini, peel the onion, and wash the mushrooms. Using a food processor with a shredder blade attached, put the zucchini and carrots through the shredder. You can also use a hand grater, but I find the food processor makes it much faster. You don't need to wash out the bowl of the food processor between each step, so save yourself the time and skip it.

3 Heat 1 tbsp of the olive oil in a large frying pan over medium heat. Peel and crush the garlic into the pan and sauté for 30 seconds. Do not allow it to burn. Add the carrots and zucchini, stir well, and sauté for about 12 minutes to draw out the moisture and cook the vegetables.

4 Once you've emptied the food processor bowl, grate or shred the mushrooms and then the onion in the same way. In a separate large frying pan, heat the remaining 1 tbsp oil over medium heat. Add the onions and mushrooms and sauté for about 5 minutes. Add the vinegar and za'atar, stir, and cook until the onions and mushrooms are fully cooked and have sweated out all their moisture. Season to taste with salt and pepper and set aside.

5 After the zucchini and carrots are cooked, add the tinned tomatoes and the Basil Purée and simmer for another 15 minutes or so. Season to taste with salt and pepper and set aside.

6 Put the spinach and ricotta into the bowl of the food processor and purée until the spinach is fully blended and the mixture is smooth. Season with salt and pepper. Grate the ball of mozzarella cheese and set aside.

7 Now you are ready to assemble the lasagna. The quantity of noodles to use is up to you. I generally only use 2 to 3 layers of noodles, as I like thick layers of veggies, but it's your lasagna, and using more noodles will extend the sauce and allow you to make a bigger pan, if desired.

8 Spread a layer of the tomato mix on the bottom of the dish, then cover with a layer of noodles, followed by the mushroom mix, the ricotta, another layer of noodles, and the remainder of the tomato mix. If you still have room in the pan and veggies to use up, do another layer, if desired.

9 Cover the pan with foil and bake in the oven for 30 to 35 minutes, then remove the foil, sprinkle with both mozzarella and Parmesan, and return to the oven for another 15 minutes or so, until the sides are bubbling and the cheese is melted. Let stand 5 to 10 minutes and serve.

SERVES 8

PECAN COCOA PUFFS

As a little girl, I loved baking, especially at Christmas. Back then, one of my favourite festive treats to make was Pecan Puffs from the *Joy of Cooking*. Fast-forward a few years and I've devised my own riff on these classic little melt-in-your-mouth sweet treats. Preparing these cocoa puffs is one of those treasured sentimental rituals that puts me in the festive spirit.

2 cups	pecans
1 bar (100 g)	Lindt dark chocolate bar, broken into pieces
1 cup	butter
1/4 cup	brown sugar
2 tsp	vanilla extract
2/3 cup	coconut
3/4 cup	all-purpose flour
1 cup	Flour Power Blend (pg 205)
1 cup	confectioners' sugar

1 Using a food processor, pulse the pecans and chocolate until they are a fine meal.

2 Add the butter, brown sugar, and vanilla and blend again until the mixture resembles whipped butter.

3 Add the coconut and pulse until well blended, then add the flours on low speed until they're mixed in (but do not overmix).

4 Remove the dough and transfer to a mixing bowl. Chill in the freezer for about 30 minutes, until the dough is cool and firm, then scoop it out with a teaspoon, roll into a ball, and place on a baking sheet lined with parchment paper. (You can put them close together, as the dough doesn't spread out much while cooking.)

5 Preheat the oven to 300°F.

6 Bake for 45 minutes, or until the cookies start to turn golden brown.

7 Once the cookies are done, remove the sheet from the oven. Using a sieve, dust the cookies with confectioners' sugar. Leave the cookies to cool, transfer to a serving plate or cookie tin, and dust lightly once more.

MAKES ABOUT 4 DOZEN COOKIES

DOUBLE-CHOCOLATE COCONUT LAVA COOKIES

Chocolate is good. Double chocolate with coconut is even better. These chocolate creations are so melt-in-your-mouth delicious that I call them "lava" cookies. Go on, try to have just one!

3/4 cup	salted butter
1/2 cup	brown sugar
1/2 cup	cane sugar
2	large eggs
1 tsp	vanilla extract
1/3 cup	unsweetened cocoa powder
1/2 cup	unsweetened, desiccated coconut
3/4 cup	cake flour
3/4 cup	Flour Power Blend (pg 205) (you can use just cake flour, if preferred, for a total of 1 1/2 cups)
1 tsp	baking soda
1/2 tsp	salt

1 Preheat the oven to 350°F.

2 Put the butter and both sugars in the bowl of an electric mixer and beat on medium-high for a few minutes until well blended, light, and fluffy.

3 Add the eggs and vanilla and whip into the butter mixture, then add the cocoa and coconut and mix on medium speed until well blended.

4 Combine the flour(s), baking soda, and salt in a bowl, then slowly add to the mixer and mix on low speed until just blended, being careful not to overmix.

5 Line a baking sheet with parchment paper and drop the batter onto the sheet using a teaspoon. For flatter cookies, dip a spoon in water and press down on the dough before baking.

6 Bake for 9 to 11 minutes. Undercooked cookies will be moist and chewy and a bit more delicate. If you prefer a crisper cookie, leave them in the oven for a few more minutes.

MAKES 3 DOZEN

FESTIVE FIZZ COCKTAIL

Kick off your next soiree with a zesty and fanciful cocktail that sets the mood for a night of fun. Made with sparkling wine or champagne with a hint of orange and a splash of pomegranate juice, this festive cocktail is as pretty as it is delicious.

1	orange
16 ounces	pomegranate juice (2 ounces per flute) (make sure you use 100% real pomegranate juice)
8 ounces	Cointreau liqueur (1 ounce per flute)
1 bottle (750 ml)	sparkling wine or champagne
	pomegranate seeds

1 Use a potato peeler to create long strips of orange zest, and place a strip in each champagne flute.

2 Add 2 ounces of the pomegranate juice and 1 ounce of the Cointreau to each glass.

3 Fill the glasses with sparkling wine or champagne.

4 Garnish with pomegranate seeds.

MAKES 8 COCKTAILS

ACKNOWLEDGEMENTS

Thanks to EVERYONE who played a part in transforming these spaces from their inspiring befores that were brimming with potential to the happily ever afters you see today. Your talents make ideas come to life. So thank you to the carpenters, tilesetters, roofers, plumbers, installers, craftspeople, painters, artisans, artists, manufacturers, sewers, upholsterers, workrooms, suppliers, shops, and movers. Thank you to my design team, TV crew, publicist, HGTV, Simon & Schuster . . . and everyone else who makes my world turn and my ideas into reality.

It may take a proverbial army to make the rooms you see in this book, but the creation of the book involved a tiny and tireless team who deserve special mention. Stacey Brandford captured the beautiful images (with help from Mikael Cosmo and Ryan Coe); Natalie Hodgins gave up her designer day job to help me chop, stir, prep, and style all the recipes; Tommy Smythe and Lindsay Mens were part of these spaces from beginning to end; Rose Pereira and I sat side by side for a month as she designed every page of the book; and then Patricia Ocampo worked through many nights to edit everything I wrote. You are all stars in my world!

THANK YOU

TOMMY SMYTHE, NATALIE HODGINS, LINDSAY MENS, KATE STUART, ALLISON WILLSON, JENNIFER GIBEAU, LAURA FREMONT

TACEY BRANDFORD, ROSE PEREIRA, MIKAEL COSMO, RYAN COE, MICHAEL GRAYDON, MARK OLSON, BJORN WALLANDER, DAWNE MARIE SHONFIELD

KEVIN HANSON, PATRICIA OCAMPO, RITA SILVA, BRENDAN MAY, OLGA LEONARDO, JAIME PUTORTI, ALEXANDRE SU, ELIZABETH WHITEHEAD, FELICIA QUON, DAVID MILLAR, NANCY PURCELL, SARAH ST. PIERRE

ALEXANDER YOUNGER, ROBIN & FIONA YOUNGER, SUSAN RICHARDSON, BENJAMIN RICHARDSON, REGINA TOLENTINO, BRIANNA MACDONALD

MICHAEL PRINI, DEB MCCAIN, RICK BOSTON, MICHAEL JOSSELYN, DANIELLE PISAREK, TARA FINLAY, LILANA NOVAKOVICH, KARA REED, ANDREA GRIFFITH, TANYA LINTON, EMILY MORGAN, CHRISTINE SHIPTON

PATRICK LEE, BILL PICA, CHRIS RUSSELL, KEN SIMPSON, PETER LAPICERELLA, JIMMY SAUNDERS, DYLAN & LANCE CRANDLES, GREG MENS, KRIS GIBSON, JIM BOTTRELL, MIKE MAESE, TONY FEO, DOMENIC LUISI, BRIAN DONOVAN, GARY SEARLE, CAMERON HUMPHREYS, EUGENE SILVA, SHARI ELSON, GREGORY KUTYLA, NOAIL OSHANA, VALERIO ZINGONE, MADELEINE LOWENBORG-FRICK, JOEL LOBLAW, ZULMIRA SAMPAIO, LEO VANEYK, ROBERT MCCLEARY

#SARAHSTYLE
#ATHOME
#ATHOMESARAHSTYLE
#MAKETHEBOOK
#LIFEOFDESIGN
#BEHINDTHESCENES
#ISLANDLIFE
#COUNTRYLIFE

FOR PRODUCT AND SOURCE INFORMATION PLEASE VISIT
SARAHRICHARDSONDESIGN.COM